# Vaccines

# Other Books in the Current Controversies Series

Alternative Therapies

Anger Management

Assisted Suicide

Disaster Response

Family Violence

Homeland Security

Human Trafficking

Media Ethics

The Rights of Animals

Smoking

# Vaccines

*Sylvia Engdahl, Book Editor*

**GREENHAVEN PRESS**
*A part of Gale, Cengage Learning*

Detroit • New York • San Francisco • New Haven, Conn • Waterville, Maine • London

Christine Nasso, *Publisher*
Elizabeth Des Chenes, *Managing Editor*

© 2009 Greenhaven Press, a part of Gale, Cengage Learning

Gale and Greenhaven Press are registered trademarks used herein under license.

*For more information, contact:*
Greenhaven Press
27500 Drake Rd.
Farmington Hills, MI 48331-3535
Or you can visit our Internet site at gale.cengage.com

For product information and technology assistance, contact us at

Gale Customer Support, 1-800-877-4253
For permission to use material from this text or product, submit all requests online at
www.cengage.com/permissions

Further permissions questions can be emailed to permissionrequest@cengage.com

Articles in Greenhaven Press anthologies are often edited for length to meet page require-ments. In addition, original titles of these works are changed to clearly present the main thesis and to explicitly indicate the author's opinion. Every effort is made to ensure that Greenhaven Press accurately reflects the original intent of the authors. Every effort has been made to trace the owners of copyrighted material.

Cover photograph reproduced by permission of Image copyright Leah-Anne Thompson, 2008. Used under license from Shutterstock.com.

**LIBRARY OF CONGRESS CATALOGING-IN-PUBLICATION DATA**

Vaccines / Sylvia Engdahl, book editor.
    p. cm. -- (Current controversies)
Includes bibliographical references and index.
ISBN-13: 978-0-7377-4150-6 (hardcover)
ISBN-13: 978-0-7377-4151-3 (pbk.)
1. Vaccination--Popular works. 2. Vaccines--Popular works. 3. Vaccination of children--Popular works. I. Engdahl, Sylvia.
  RA638.V333 2009
  614.4'7083--dc22

                                                    2008031422

Printed in the United States of America
1 2 3 4 5 6 7 12 11 10 09 08

# Contents

Foreword                                                             13

Introduction                                                         16

## Chapter 1: Are Vaccines Likely to Do More Harm than Good?

Overview: Opposition to Childhood                                    21
Vaccinations Is Increasing
  *Mike Cronin*

  A growing number of parents believe that vaccines are
  harmful, but doctors and public health officials say this
  view is unfounded and potentially catastrophic.

### Yes: The Risks of Common Vaccines Often Exceed Their Benefits

There Are Real Dangers to Vaccines                                   26
  *David Kupelian*

  Vaccines have saved many lives but they have dangerous
  side effects. As such, parents should learn about each
  vaccine and consider carefully whether the risk is warranted in the case of their own children.

Vaccines May Be the Cause of Autism                                  32
  *Kelly Patricia O'Meara*

  Mercury is known to be dangerous and it still may be
  present in some vaccines. Despite official denials, there is
  evidence that mercury has caused autism.

Some Parents Feel They Must Lie to Avoid                             40
Vaccination of Their Children
  *Steve LeBlanc*

  Some parents falsely claim religious objections to vaccination in order that their children will be exempted from
  getting the vaccines under the law, when their real objec-
  tion is that they believe vaccines are unsafe.

Many Scientific Studies of Vaccine Safety     **45**
Are Flawed

*Robert F. Kennedy Jr.*

Mothers who oppose vaccination are not irrational; they are making an informed decision to protect their children from "Thimerosal-laced vaccines" in the face of opposition from government bureaucrats, public health officials, and the vaccine industry.

The Cervical Cancer Vaccine Has Not Been     **49**
Proven Safe or Effective

*Cathy Gulli, Lianne George, and John Intini*

Not enough is known about the long-term effects of the new HPV (human papilloma virus) vaccine, Gardasil, for it to be given to a generation of young girls, especially when cervical cancer can be easily detected and cured.

**No: The Risk of Harm from Common
Vaccines Is Extremely Small**

The Benefits of Vaccines Far Outweigh     **58**
the Risks

*Aubrey Noelle Stimola*

Fears of side effects from childhood vaccines as reported by the media carry too much weight with parents, most of whom have no experience with the diseases vaccines prevent. These vaccines have saved million of lives, and their proven safety and effectiveness over the past decades should prompt parents to get vaccinations and not opt out due to unfounded fears of vaccine-related illnesses.

Giving Multiple Vaccines to Children Is Safe     **64**

*Centers for Disease Control and Prevention*

It is untrue that giving many different vaccines at the same time can overload a child's immune system. Babies need as much protection as possible during their first few months of life, and simultaneous giving of a combination of vaccines ensures that they receive the immunization when they need it most while having to endure fewer injections.

Anti-Vaccine Fanatics Are Free Riders                      68
  *Michael Fumento*

  Fanatical opponents of vaccination are freeloaders who
  benefit from the fact that childhood diseases have been
  wiped out by vaccination, but who feel no public obliga-
  tion of vaccinating their own children. If too many parents are scared into refusing vaccination of their children, these diseases will return.

## Chapter 2: Should Routine Vaccinations Be Mandatory?

Overview: Vaccination Controversy Centers                 75
on the Right to Choose
  *Logan Molyneux*

  Much of the resistance to vaccination occurs because it is
  compulsory. Opponents believe that they have a right to
  choose whether or not to vaccinate their children,
  whereas public health officials maintain that if many of
  them opt out, eradicated diseases will reappear.

### Yes: Vaccination Should Be Mandatory in Order to Prevent the Spread of Disease

Meningitis Vaccination Should Be                          81
Mandatory for College Dorm Residents
  *Katie Strickland*

  Meningitis is a dangerous disease, and too few people are
  aware of the risk. Vaccination should be required for all
  incoming college students, particularly those who want
  to live in dorms.

All Young Girls Should Be Vaccinated to                   84
Prevent Cervical Cancer
  *Elizabeth M. Whelan*

  Vaccination is a medical matter, not a moral one, and religious objections to vaccinating girls against HPV
  (human papilloma virus) are not a valid reason for opposing it.

## No: Mandatory Vaccination Violates People's Right to Control Their Bodies

Making Cervical Cancer Vaccination                    87
Mandatory Is Bad Medicine
*Lucinda Marshall*

The cervical cancer vaccine Gardasil is being promoted by the pharmaceutical company that produces it, Merck & Co., although its safety is unproven. It is wrong for states to require that young girls get the vaccine for the sake of preventing a treatable cancer that can be prevented by other means.

The Chickenpox Vaccine Is Unnecessary                 91
and Its Safety Is Unproven
*Andrew Schlafly*

Chickenpox is not a dangerous disease, but the vaccine sometimes has harmful side effects. As such, children should not be forced to undergo unnecessary inoculation against the disease, as is being mandated or considered by a number of states.

New Jersey's New Childhood Vaccine                     96
Mandates Are Indefensible
*Deirdre Imus*

A number of vaccines contain mercury, which is toxic, and these vaccines should not be required for preschool children, as is being proposed by public health officials in New Jersey. Until the safety of these vaccines is improved, parents, not government, should determine if and when they are given.

Compulsory Vaccination Eliminates Normal              104
Checks on Government Power
*Mark Blaxill and Barbara Loe Fisher*

The chance of negligence and incompetence in vaccination programs increases when democratic checks and balances, and the longstanding medical practice of "informed consent," are removed by making these programs compulsory.

Push to Mandate New Vaccines Comes         **110**
from Profit-Driven Industry

*Evelyn Pringle*

The addition of new vaccines to the mandatory schedules is the result of promotion by the pharmaceutical industry. Moreover, studies have shown that booster shots
of older vaccines are not needed as often as has been
thought, and that such unnecessary overdosing with vaccines can cause harm.

## Chapter 3: Does the Threat of Bioterrorism Warrant Mandatory Vaccination?

Chapter Preface         **119**

### Yes: Vaccination Against Biological Weapons Is Essential to Defense

Anthrax Vaccine Is Necessary to Protect         **122**
Services Members

*Stephanie L. Carl*

Anthrax vaccination is essential to protect armed services
members from biological attacks by terrorists in the field.

High-Risk Situations Justify Government         **125**
Restrictions on Liberty

*Lawrence O. Gostin*

The government unquestionably has the power to restrict
liberty for the sake of community safety in situations
where the risk is great enough to justify the means employed; for example, a bioterror attack that caused a
public health emergency would warrant mandatory vaccination, quarantines, etc.

**No: Unproven Vaccines Can Cause Harm
and Should Not Be Forced on Anyone**

Service Members Should Not Be Ordered                    **136**
to Risk Damage to Their Health
  *Bob Evans*

  It is not right for service members to be forced to choose
  between risking their health by accepting unsafe vaccines,
  such as the anthrax vaccination, or being punished for
  disobeying orders.

Mandatory Anthrax Vaccination Has                        **140**
Caused Many Serious Illnesses
  *Greg Gordon*

  Many civilian contractors and military personnel have
  developed serious illnesses from the anthrax vaccine,
  which was compulsory for certain service personnel until
  2004. Although questions still remain about the safety of
  the vaccine, the U.S. government announced in late 2006
  that it would resume its mandatory program for service
  members being deployed to high-risk areas such as Iraq,
  Afghanistan, and South Korea.

Compulsory Vaccination Against Bioterrorist              **147**
Attacks Is Unjustified
  *Tom Jefferson*

  The medical evidence for the safety and effectiveness of
  smallpox and anthrax vaccines is not sufficient to justify
  making them compulsory when the extent of the threat
  is unknown.

## Chapter 4: What Are Some Future Uses for Vaccines?

Chapter Preface                                          **152**

Lives Could Be Saved by More Vaccination                 **154**
of Adolescents and Adults
  *Steve Baragona*

  Many people assume that vaccination is necessary only
  for children, and some adults needlessly die or become
  seriously ill from diseases that could be prevented by
  adult vaccination.

Measles Is a Major Cause of Death Among      157
Unvaccinated Children in Africa
  *William J. Moss*
  Many children in Africa still die of measles, although in
  areas where vaccination and monitoring have been implemented, the situation is improving. Wider vaccinations
  would save many more children.

Children Infected with HIV Need Access      162
to Pneumonia Vaccine
  *Orin Levine and Paul Zeitz*
  Children who are HIV-positive are especially vulnerable
  to pneumonia. In rich countries they are protected by
  vaccination, but in developing countries they die from
  pneumococcal infections. Many lives could be saved if
  the vaccine for pneumonia were made available in the
  developing world.

More Women Should Be Enrolled in      165
HIV Preventive Vaccine Trials
  *Edward Mills, Stephanie Nixon, Sonal Singh,*
  *Sonam Dolma, Anjali Nayyar, and Sushma Kapoor*
  Comparatively few women in developing countries have
  participated in trials of HIV vaccines because there are
  cultural barriers to their doing so. It is important to find
  ways to encourage them so that a vaccine that is effective
  for women can be developed.

Experimental AIDS Vaccines Have Not      173
Been Successful
  *John Lauerman*
  Late in 2007, the trial of a promising AIDS vaccine had
  to be stopped because the vaccine may actually increase
  people's susceptibility to HIV rather than protect against
  it. Other HIV vaccine research will continue nonetheless.

A Malaria Vaccine Is Desperately Needed      177
in Africa
  *Michael Finkel*
  Malaria threatens half the world's population and deaths
  from the disease, especially of children, are increasing.
  For many years scientists have been seeking a malaria
  vaccine, but it is more difficult to develop than other
  vaccines.

Vaccines Are Being Developed to                    **184**
Treat Cancer
  *Michelle Meadows*

  Although the usual purpose of vaccination is to prevent
  disease, scientists are finding that vaccines can also be
  used to make the body's immune system attack cancer
  cells.

New Vaccines May Help to Stop Smoking,             **193**
Drug Use, and Overeating
  *Ronald Kotulak*

  Scientists are now developing new kinds of vaccines that
  may make it easier for people to overcome habits and
  addictions that are dangerous to their health.

Organizations to Contact                           **198**

Bibliography                                       **206**

Index                                              **212**

# Foreword

By definition, controversies are "discussions of questions in which opposing opinions clash" (Webster's Twentieth Century Dictionary Unabridged). Few would deny that controversies are a pervasive part of the human condition and exist on virtually every level of human enterprise. Controversies transpire between individuals and among groups, within nations and between nations. Controversies supply the grist necessary for progress by providing challenges and challengers to the status quo. They also create atmospheres where strife and warfare can flourish. A world without controversies would be a peaceful world; but it also would be, by and large, static and prosaic.

## The Series' Purpose

The purpose of the Current Controversies series is to explore many of the social, political, and economic controversies dominating the national and international scenes today. Titles selected for inclusion in the series are highly focused and specific. For example, from the larger category of criminal justice, Current Controversies deals with specific topics such as police brutality, gun control, white collar crime, and others. The debates in Current Controversies also are presented in a useful, timeless fashion. Articles and book excerpts included in each title are selected if they contribute valuable, long-range ideas to the overall debate. And wherever possible, current information is enhanced with historical documents and other relevant materials. Thus, while individual titles are current in focus, every effort is made to ensure that they will not become quickly outdated. Books in the Current Controversies series will remain important resources for librarians, teachers, and students for many years.

In addition to keeping the titles focused and specific, great care is taken in the editorial format of each book in the series. Book introductions and chapter prefaces are offered to provide background material for readers. Chapters are organized around several key questions that are answered with diverse opinions representing all points on the political spectrum. Materials in each chapter include opinions in which authors clearly disagree as well as alternative opinions in which authors may agree on a broader issue but disagree on the possible solutions. In this way, the content of each volume in Current Controversies mirrors the mosaic of opinions encountered in society. Readers will quickly realize that there are many viable answers to these complex issues. By questioning each author's conclusions, students and casual readers can begin to develop the critical thinking skills so important to evaluating opinionated material.

Current Controversies is also ideal for controlled research. Each anthology in the series is composed of primary sources taken from a wide gamut of informational categories including periodicals, newspapers, books, U.S. and foreign government documents, and the publications of private and public organizations. Readers will find factual support for reports, debates, and research papers covering all areas of important issues. In addition, an annotated table of contents, an index, a book and periodical bibliography, and a list of organizations to contact are included in each book to expedite further research.

Perhaps more than ever before in history, people are confronted with diverse and contradictory information. During the Persian Gulf War, for example, the public was not only treated to minute-to-minute coverage of the war, it was also inundated with critiques of the coverage and countless analyses of the factors motivating U.S. involvement. Being able to sort through the plethora of opinions accompanying today's major issues, and to draw one's own conclusions, can be a complicated and frustrating struggle. It is the editors' hope that Current Controversies will help readers with this struggle.

# Introduction

> "*The issue of whether vaccines cause illness is not settled. The vast majority of scientists and physicians feel sure that they do not, except in rare cases of people who are allergic. . . . [But] it is impossible to state categorically either that vaccination is safe or that it is hazardous—though people on both sides of the debate often do so.*"

Vaccination, once routinely accepted by Americans, has become increasingly controversial in recent years. Public health experts maintain that this is because vaccination programs are victims of their own success. When diseases for which vaccines now exist were prevalent, the public feared those diseases, but now that they have been virtually eliminated, the fear has shifted to the vaccines themselves. Most people agree that it is a good idea to be vaccinated when there is an epidemic. But when the chance of contracting a disease is small, they question whether the risk of being harmed by a vaccine, rather than being helped by it, is greater. That question is being hotly debated today. The answer depends, of course, on whether or not vaccines are dangerous. Medical authorities say no. But a growing number of parents—though still a small minority—feel that vaccines can cause harm.

Searching the Internet for information on vaccination can create a false impression about the dangers of vaccines, mainly because opponents of vaccination are much more vocal and politically active than supporters. For example, in 2007, when University of Toronto researchers analyzed 153 videos about vaccination and immunization on the video-sharing Web site YouTube, they found that more than half of the videos portrayed childhood, human papillomavirus, flu, and other vaccines negatively or ambiguously. And nearly half of those videos contained messages that contradict both Canadian and American national immunization guidelines. "YouTube is increasingly a resource people consult for health information, including vaccination," said Jennifer Keelan, an assistant professor in the University of Toronto's Department of Public Health Sciences. "Our study shows that a significant amount of immunization content on YouTube contradicts the best scientific evidence at large. From a public health perspective, this is very concerning."

The Toronto research team also found that videos skeptical of vaccination received more views and better ratings by YouTube users than those that portray vaccination in a positive light. This is because videos that oppose something are often alarming presentations that rely on emotional appeal, something also true of Web sites that oppose vaccination. In 2002, the *Journal of the American Medical Association* reported on a study in which twenty-two such sites were evaluated. All of them suggested that vaccines cause illnesses, such as autism, though medical research has found no link between standard childhood vaccines and autism. Many sites also claimed that vaccines damage the immune system. A great number included personal accounts by parents of children, along with pictures of those children, whose deaths or serious illnesses they blamed on vaccines.

Supporters of vaccination point out that because the diseases vaccines prevent have been virtually wiped out in the United States, there are no comparable stories and pictures of children suffering from these diseases, which would provide the public with a balanced story. Sites that advocate vaccination show healthy children and state that vaccines enable them to stay healthy. For the same reasons that the media can attract bigger audiences with bad news than with good, people are prone to pay more attention to alleged injury from vaccination than to its proven benefits.

The fact that a point of view is based more on emotion than on science, however, does not necessarily mean that its content is untrue. The issue of whether vaccines cause illness is not settled. The vast majority of scientists and physicians feel sure that they do not, except in rare cases of people who are allergic. There have been many scientific trials that show vaccines are safe. But it is extremely difficult to design and conduct a trial in which all variables are taken into account. There is no way to be absolutely sure that the results of a trial are valid for all people, and critics often point out what they believe to be flaws in these studies. So it is impossible to state categorically either that vaccination is safe or that it is hazard-ous—though people on both sides of the debate often do so.

There is another important issue in the debate over vacci-nation. An increasing number of people feel that mandatory vaccination is a violation of their civil liberties. They believe citizens should be allowed to decide whether or not to have their children vaccinated, just as they have the right, under the law, to choose or refuse other forms of medical treatment. Both the ethical and the emotional nature of this issue fuels the anti-vaccination movement; some people who have no ob-jection to vaccination on health grounds strongly object to it being compulsory. In contrast, public health authorities be-lieve that if childhood vaccination were not mandatory, seri-ous infectious diseases would make a resurgence and that the government has a right to prevent threats to the broader pub-lic health even if it means depriving people of their individual rights in this matter.

Although the law cannot compel adults to be forcibly vac-cinated or to permit vaccination of their children, there are penalties for those who refuse to comply. Children who are not vaccinated can be kept out of school or denied other pub-lic benefits, and according to the famous Supreme Court case *Jacobson v. Commonwealth of Massachusetts* (1905), which re-mains the legal basis for compulsory vaccination, it is not unconstitutional for people to be fined or put in jail for refusing to obey vaccination laws. In November 2007, parents of more than twenty-three hundred Maryland children were told that if they did not bring their children to the courthouse on a day set for mass vaccination, they would be fined $50 or jailed. This event created a storm of protest on the Internet. Reflecting a widespread feeling among anti-vaccination groups, Barbara Loe Fisher, a noted opponent of vaccination, wrote, "Limiting the power of the State to force vaccination is all that stands between the people and tyranny. There is only one way we will be free in the future: the laws must be changed so that every state allows a conscientious belief exemption to vaccination."

Most states do allow religious—and in some cases, philosophical—exemptions, and the movement toward extending such laws is growing. On the other hand, opposition to them is also on the rise. Public health officials are disturbed by the fact that fewer children are receiving vaccinations and have proposed making exemptions harder to obtain. Some officials have even suggested that homeschooling parents who fail to get their children vaccinated should be prosecuted for child neglect.

There is no simple solution to the vaccination controversy. A satisfactory balance between public health considerations and individual rights will be difficult to achieve. However, when seeking such a balance, it is wise to remember that all arguments about the subject are based at least partially on opinion—and that in judging opinions, allowances have to be made for the amount of emotion with which they are expressed.

# Chapter 1

# Are Vaccines Likely to Do More Harm than Good?

# Overview: Opposition to Childhood Vaccination Is Increasing

*Mike Cronin*

*Mike Cronin is a reporter for the* Pittsburgh Tribune-Review.

Elena Neil's oldest daughter already showed symptoms of autism by the time Neil learned that Pennsylvania allowed parents to claim a religious exemption from mandatory vaccinations of their children.

Fever and rashes afflicted Gina, now 9, each time she received a vaccination, her mother said. But when Gina became reclusive and introverted after five vaccinations in one day when she was about 15 months old, Neil wondered if those treatments were causing her daughter's health problems.

Several years of naturopathic treatments have rid Gina of her neurological disorder symptoms, her mother said. Yet she is allergic to penicillin, peanuts, wheat and gluten and has asthma. Neil said she believes the vaccinations caused these maladies.

"People look at me like I'm crazy because I've never had Olivia vaccinated," Neil, 40, said about her second daughter, who is 5. "But she's had nothing of what Gina has."

## Parents Are Wary of Vaccines

Many parents believe vaccinations against diseases such as measles, diphtheria, mumps and chicken pox pose a danger to children because the serums contain ingredients such as mercury and aluminum. More Pennsylvania parents are choosing not to vaccinate their children.

Mike Cronin, "Pennsylvania Parents Grow Wary of Vaccines," *Pittsburgh Tribune-Review*, November 5, 2007. Images and text copyright © 2007 by The Tribune-Review Publishing Co. Reproduced by permission.

The number of students in Pennsylvania claiming religious or medical exemptions from vaccinations has more than doubled in the past eight years—to 24,919 [in 2006] from 9,722 in 1999, according to the state Department of Health.

Jeanne Truschel, 37, a speech pathologist, said her daughter Calla, 3, has never had a vaccination.

"I was really alarmed to learn about how many vaccines infants get in the first 24 months of their lives," Truschel said. "I didn't want her to be exposed to all those toxins. And she's completely healthy. She's never even had a runny nose."

## Diseases Are "a Plane Ride Away"

Doctors and public health officials counter that this attitude is unfounded, immoral and potentially catastrophic.

"It's unconscionable not to vaccinate your kids," said Dr. Toni Darville, chief of infectious diseases at Children's Hospital of Pittsburgh. "You have to have the moral grounding so you not only protect your child, but others as well. Especially with plane travel universal. Any of the serious infectious diseases are essentially a plane ride away."

Darville said some diseases—such as whooping cough in England and Japan and mumps in New York and Iowa—have reappeared because of falling vaccination rates.

"As diseases go away, people aren't aware of how horrible it can be, so there's no impetus to say, 'Oh my God,'" Darville said. "All these diseases can cause severe symptoms and even death."

## Link to Autism Studied

Dr. Samuel Stebbins, professor and researcher with the University of Pittsburgh's Center for Vaccine Research, called vaccines "the single most effective public health intervention available" but said he supports "parents' right and responsibility to question the 'system' and to make informed choices."

At the start of the 20th century, a third of deaths in the United States were from infectious diseases, Stebbins said. The average life expectancy for those born in 1900 was 47.3 [years], according to the Centers for Disease Control and Prevention [CDC] in Atlanta.

By 2004, life expectancy had reached 77.8. Citing other CDC data, Stebbins said cases and deaths from diseases such as smallpox, polio and measles have plummeted during the past 100 years.

---

*All vaccines except those for flu have been mercury-free since 2002.*

---

Yet Stebbins concedes his mind remains open about the causes for the mushrooming rate of autism in American children, though he believes the causes likely are environmental toxins and genetic susceptibility. In 1987, the autism rate was one in 10,000, reported journalist David Kirby in his book, *Evidence of Harm*, which investigated the link between autism and mercury in vaccines. The book was honored in 2005 for outstanding investigative reporting by the nonprofit organization Investigative Reporters and Editors.

A CDC study published in February [2007] said about one child in 150 develops autism or a related disorder by the age of 8.

Federal public health officials recommended—but did not ban—phasing out the use of thimerosal, a mercury preservative, in vaccines in the late 1990s. CDC spokesman Curtis Allen said officials made that decision based on "an abundance of caution," and all vaccines except those for flu have been mercury-free since 2002. The mercury preservative allows easier storage by enabling the production of multi-dose vaccine vials, Allen said. People can request thimerosal-free flu shots.

CDC and U.S. Food and Drug Administration [FDA] officials point to studies that show no connection between mercury and autism.

But Dr. Mark Geier, 59, a private practitioner who has worked for the National Institutes of Health, and his son, David Geier, 27, of Silver Spring, Md., said that after conducting more than 25 independent studies, they believe there is a relationship between mercury and autism.

The Geiers published a paper [in 2006] in the peer-reviewed journal *Neuroendocrinology Letters* that examined side effects in patients who collectively received about 100 million doses of vaccines between 1994 and 2000.

They found "significant risks of autism, speech disorders, mental retardation, personality disorders, thinking abnormalities, ataxia, and neurodevelopmental delays in general were associated with mercury exposure from thimerosal-containing childhood vaccines." Ataxia is an unsteadiness and lack of coordination, generally caused by a brain disease.

## "Not Just the Vaccine"

Dr. Sherri Tenpenny of Cleveland, a specialist in emergency medicine and osteopathic manipulation who has researched vaccinations, unapologetically opposes all vaccinations because of more than 100 toxins beyond mercury—such as aluminum and polysorbate 80—that can be found in vaccines. Tenpenny argues the benefits of vaccines are outweighed by the neurological disorders and other illnesses caused by the frequency of vaccinations and the accumulation of the toxins they contain.

"When you look at the fact that we're the most highly vaccinated population in the world, yet we are sickest, in dollars spent, something is wrong with public health in this country," Tenpenny said. "I believe it's morally wrong to compel someone against their will to inject their children with substances that have potential to kill them."

Julie Hudak, 39, owns a business that provides occupational, speech and other therapies to 26 children a week who have developmental disabilities including autism. Hudak has three children, 20 months, 4 and 6. All have received the traditional course of vaccinations. None has any neurological disorders.

"I believe in vaccines because the risk of epidemics breaking out because of people not getting them is scary," Hudak said.

She acknowledged, however, that children who are genetically predisposed to conditions such as autism and who suffer from environmental toxins could "be pushed over the edge" after receiving a certain vaccine.

"It's not just the vaccine that causes autism," she said.

# There Are Real Dangers to Vaccines

*David Kupelian*

*David Kupelian is vice president and managing editor of World-NetDaily.com and* Whistleblower *magazine, the author of a best-selling book, and a speaker who has been featured on many television programs.*

It wasn't until right after the little girl had received her third and final pertussis shot that all hell broke loose. One of five children in a Christian homeschooling family I know well, the child suffered an extreme and life-altering reaction to the common childhood vaccine. Today, perhaps 15 years later, her family's life largely revolves around taking care of the now-teenage girl, confined to a wheelchair, unable to speak, her life decimated by a "required" vaccine shot.

Indeed, the National Vaccine Injury Compensation Program, part of the federal Department of Health and Human Services, was set up years ago to pay for the care of just such vaccine-injured Americans. If you or your child suffers from anaphylactic shock or brachial neuritis as a result of getting any tetanus-toxoid-containing vaccine, you're eligible. Develop encephalopathy—literally, disease of the brain—from pertussis antigen–containing vaccines, or from measles, mumps and rubella virus–containing vaccines, and you qualify. What about chronic arthritis from rubella virus-containing vaccines, or a vaccine-strain measles viral infection from a measles virus–containing vaccine?

What about contracting paralytic polio or vaccine-strain polio viral infection from a polio live virus–containing vaccine, or intussusception (prolapsed intestine) from vaccines containing live, oral, rhesus-based rotavirus?

These are just some of the vaccine-caused injuries suffered by Americans, conditions quietly being cared for with federal dollars.

## The Vaccine Debate

To report journalistically on vaccination controversies is a real challenge. On one side you have the medical establishment, including the federal government's Centers for Disease Control and Prevention [CDC], which endlessly repeats the mantra that vaccines are safe and effective and everybody should get them. To question their wisdom makes you a paranoid conspiracy theorist.

On the other hand, you have a substantial and growing movement of skeptics, including many medical professionals, who openly question vaccines. Some are strident, claiming all vaccines are bad for all people at all times and places, and a few even impute a sinister motive to vaccine manufacturers and the doctors that give the shots. But many others are careful and nuanced and very well informed. They consider each vaccine individually on its merits as well as its known and suspected negatives—and still come out holding up a big "caution" sign.

---

*Vaccines have saved countless lives. They also have a history of disastrous side effects and suspected or proven dangers.*

---

For years, the vaccine debate was confined largely to the traditional childhood vaccines like DPT (diphtheria-pertussis-tetanus), MMR (measles-mumps-rubella) and polio. Even then, there were major concerns. The pertussis vaccine, for example, is notorious for having rare but horrendous side effects, and most polio cases in the world in recent years have been caused by the live-virus vaccine itself! These are widely known facts the CDC will not contradict—although it certainly doesn't go out of its way to advertise the dark side of vaccines. (The U.S. government stopped using the live-virus polio vaccine in 2000 because of the incidents of vaccine-related polio, the last U.S. case of which was documented in 1999.)

But in recent times, many new childhood vaccines have been introduced, from rotavirus and chickenpox to hepatitis B, meningitis and pneumonia, each with their own controversies and, in some cases, scandals. At first, the new vaccines are just "suggested," then they became "recommended" by pediatricians, and before long they're "required" before entering public school.

## Problems with New Vaccines

As a result of all this vaccine-mania:

- Right now, state after state is attempting literally to force young, prepubescent school-girls into getting a brand-new vaccine, with an unproven safety record, to prevent a sexually transmitted form of cancer. The manufacturer, pharmaceutical giant Merck, has lobbied state politicians to make their vaccine mandatory. It is as though we assume all these girls will act like prostitutes in a few years. (Indeed, one can easily argue that forcing girls to take this shot would serve to *encourage* risky and immoral sexual behavior, as they might feel protected from the consequences of such activity.)

- Surprise, WND [World Net Daily] reported at least three deaths and more than 1,600 adverse reactions including spontaneous abortion and paralysis . . . connected to the Merck vaccine, called Gardasil.

- There's major movement toward an AIDS vaccine. Once approved by the government, will there be another push like the current one to immunize school-girls against a sexually transmitted disease, only this time to mandate the AIDS vaccine for everybody?

- Despite publicity to the contrary, the controversial mercury-based vaccine preservative Thimerosal— thought by some researchers to be linked to rising levels of autism in the U.S.—is still used in some vaccines.

- WND has documented the forced vaccination of a newborn against a sexually transmitted disease, despite the parents' strenuous objections, with armed guards present to ensure the infant's inoculation.

- Can vaccines cause cancer? Between 1955 and 1963, some *10 to 30 million Americans* received polio shots tainted with Simian virus 40, or SV40, a monkey virus now known to be associated with certain forms of cancer in humans. Sound too bizarre and conspiratorial to believe? You can read it right on the website of the federal government's Centers for Disease Control and Prevention.

- Then there's the U.S. military, which compels soldiers to get multiple vaccinations. Some experts, citing compelling evidence, blame the military's anthrax shots for the epidemic dubbed "Gulf War Syndrome."

---

*Most "health officials" concerned with immunology are not focused on what is best for you and your individual child, but on what they perceive to be the best interests of the population as a whole.*

---

Despite all the negatives, the subject of vaccines is not black and white, although both sides in the controversy tend to make the issue sound that way. The truth is, vaccines have saved countless lives. They also have a history of disastrous side effects and suspected or proven dangers—a dark downside utterly covered up by the public health establishment.

So, I'm not going to advise you that "Vaccines A, B and C are bad—don't get them. Vaccines D and E are good—get them."

## Research the Subject for Yourselves

Rather, the purpose of this column is to begin to expose you to the rest of the vaccine story—the part you never hear about from other media. An unfortunate mindset permeates the medical world (and elsewhere) with the message that citizens are either too ignorant, uneducated or just plain dumb to do their own research and come to their own conclusions. Yet this is one area where each of us must do just that. If you have young children, you need to research for yourself the subject of vaccines and look at each on its merits.

For instance, many will tell you the vaccine to regard with the most suspicion would be pertussis, due to the disastrous outcome that sometimes results. On the other end of the spectrum, tetanus seems to evoke the least concern about side effects, and to confer the most tangible benefits, especially if you live in a farm area and work with animals.

The bottom line is that all of us need to research this subject with an open and critical mind. Vaccine decisions can be difficult, as you attempt to balance the promised benefits with known and suspected negative effects. Along with obtaining good information, we have to consider our particular situation. And intuition also plays a vital role.

It's critical to understand clearly that most "health officials" concerned with immunology are *not* focused on what is best for you and your individual child, but on what they perceive to be the best interests of the population as a whole. And from that macro viewpoint, they strive to maintain what they call the "herd immunity." In other words, if large numbers of people opt out of vaccination, even for the most wholesome and sensible of reasons, the medical establishment will oppose it out of fear that once-eradicated (like smallpox) or near-eradicated (like polio) diseases will come back.

And yet, because there are *real dangers* to vaccines, we owe it to our children, to ourselves and to God to become informed, and then make our decisions based on what is truly right for us, not on other people's notions of what they think serves the collective good. They might well be wrong.

Remember, despite the medical establishment's paramount concern over "herd immunity," we are not cattle.

# Vaccines May Be the Cause of Autism

*Kelly Patricia O'Meara*

*Kelly Patricia O'Meara is an investigative reporter for* Insight on the News, *a weekly newsmagazine.*

The mother of an autistic child wonders aloud when health officials will wake up to the epidemic that has claimed not only her son but hundreds of thousands of other children in the United States, with no end in sight. She muses, "Maybe someday this will be as important as SARS [severe acute respiratory syndrome] and we'll get the same attention. God knows we need it."

Autism is a severely incapacitating developmental disability for which there is no known cure. According to a recently released report by the California Department of Developmental Services, or DDS, entitled "Autistic Spectrum Disorders, Changes in the California Caseload: 1999–2002", the rate of children diagnosed with full-syndrome autism in the Golden State between 1999 and 2002 nearly doubled from 10,360 to 20,377. The report further revealed that "between Dec. 31, 1987, and Dec. 31, 2002, the population of persons with full-syndrome autism has increased by 634 percent." That is a doubling of autism cases every four years, and the staggering increases are not limited to California. According to data provided by the U.S. Department of Education, the increased autism rate in California is in line with the increases other states are experiencing. . . .

## Harmful Vaccine Ingredients?

For years there has been a debate about the cause or causes of autism, but the vast majority of finger-pointing has been directed at childhood vaccines as the culprit. And considering what is put into the vaccines injected into hours-old infants, it is easy to understand why they are at the top of the list of suspects: formaldehyde (used in embalming), thimerosal (nearly 50 percent mercury), aluminum phosphate (toxic and carcinogenic), antibiotics, phenols (corrosive to skin and toxic), aluminum salts (corrosive to tissue and neurotoxic), methanol (toxic), isopropyl (toxic), 2-pheoxyethanol (toxic), live viruses and a host of unknown components considered off-limits as trade secrets. These are just part of the vaccine mixture.

For those who believe there are elements in vaccines that may be responsible for the increased number of autism cases and other neurological disorders, thimerosal currently is at the top of the list of possible culprits being investigated.

---

*It is no secret among government and health officials that mercury is toxic and causes serious adverse reactions.*

---

Despite official insistence that the evidence linking injected thimerosal to autism is inconclusive, the data suggest otherwise. In 1999 the National Academy of Sciences Institute of Medicine (IOM) must have thought there was something seriously wrong when it supported removal of thimerosal from vaccines, stating that it was "a prudent measure in support of the public goal to reduce mercury exposure of infants and children as much as possible." The IOM further urged that "full consideration be given to removing thimerosal from any biological product to which infants, children and pregnant women are exposed."

## Mercury Exceeds Safety Guidelines

A recently published study in the *Journal of American Physicians and Surgeons* by Mark Geier, M.D., Ph.D., and president of the Genetic Centers of America and his son, David Geier, president of Medcon Inc. and a consultant on vaccine cases, was titled "Thimerosal in Childhood Vaccines, Neurodevelopment Disorders and Heart Disease in the United States." It presents strong epidemiological evidence for a link between neurodevelopmental disorders and mercury exposure from thimerosal-containing childhood vaccines.

Specifically, the authors evaluated the doses of mercury that children received as part of their immunization schedule, then compared these doses with federal safety guidelines....

The authors concluded that "in light of voluminous literature supporting the biologic mechanisms for mercury-induced adverse reactions, the presence of amounts of mercury in thimerosal-containing childhood vaccines exceeding federal safety guidelines for the oral ingestion of mercury and previous epidemiological studies showing adverse reactions to such vaccines, a causal relationship between thimerosal-containing childhood vaccines and neurodevelopment disorders and heart disease appears to be confirmed."

It is no secret among government and health officials that mercury is toxic and causes serious adverse reactions. In July 1999 the American Academy of Pediatrics and the U.S. Public Health Service issued a joint statement calling for the removal of thimerosal from vaccines. Five years after the joint statement, however, it still is difficult for parents and physicians to be sure that the pharmaceutical companies have indeed removed the toxic substance from their vaccines....

Geier [states], "In addition, the influenza vaccine that is recommended for an increasing segment of the pediatric population in the U.S. also contains 25 micrograms of mercury. Assuming that the labeling is correct, it is possible that children in the U.S. in 2003 may be exposed to levels of mercury from thimerosal contained in childhood vaccines that are at higher levels than at any time in the past. Possible total childhood mercury in 2003 is more than 300 micrograms."

## Incorrect Package Labeling

Whether the "labeling is correct" is the question du jour. According to Len Lavenda, a spokesman for Aventis Pasteur, the maker of DTaP [diphtheria, tetanus, and acellular pertussis vaccine], "Aventis only sells the DTaP vaccine in the preservative-free formulation. The PDR [*Physicians' Desk Reference*] references both the single and multidose. However, when we received the license for the preservative-free we ceased sales of the multidose vial. For some reason, the package insert takes much longer to revise than one would expect."
. . .

Parents don't have to worry about their children being administered 25 micrograms of thimerosal. It just takes time to get the paperwork caught up. The current package insert does not accurately reflect what is being marketed.

Geier is astounded by Lavenda's admission. "If this is true, they should be in jail. They can't have an insert on a drug that is totally wrong. It is against all regulations. If I'm a doctor and I'm giving you a shot and the insert says such and such is in the shot, it had better be in it. If doctors can't rely on the instructions that come with what we're injecting then all bets are off. This is a far worse admission than admitting that thimerosal is still in the vaccine. There are at least 15 laws that say the insert has to match what is in the product. This is absolutely horrendous. In my entire career in medicine I have never heard of a drug company claiming that what's in the insert and the accompanying product don't match. This is total mislabeling and fraud by their own admission. Legally they should be forced to close down because our clinical decisions are based on their labeling."

Assuming that the package inserts are correct, Geier tells *Insight*, "The EPA [Environmental Protection Agency] limit is 0.1 micrograms of mercury per kilogram body weight per day. It doesn't take a genius to do the calculations when on their day of birth children are given the hepatitis B vaccine, which is 12.5 micrograms of mercury. The average newborn weighs between 6 and 7 pounds, so they would be allowed 0.3 micrograms of mercury but in this one shot they are getting 12.5 micrograms. That's 39 times more than allowed by law. And it gets worse when you consider that children are getting multiple vaccinations at 2 months. And this limit is for oral ingestion and not injection, which is much worse."

Rhonda Smith, a spokeswoman for the federal Centers for Disease Control and Prevention (CDC), tells *Insight* that, except for mere traces, thimerosal has been removed. "All routinely recommended licensed vaccines," says Smith, "that are currently being manufactured for children in the U.S., except influenza, contain no thimerosal or only trace amounts, a concentration of less than 0.0002 percent." But according to the 2003 immunization schedule and the package inserts, there appear to be a number of childhood vaccines that still contain mercury, including those for tetanus and diphtheria.

---

*If everyone acknowledges the toxicity of mercury and top U.S. health officials have called for its removal, why is thimerosal still in vaccines?*

---

This scenario becomes even more bizarre when one further considers that thimerosal is not a necessary component in vaccines. It first was introduced by pharmaceutical giant Eli Lilly and Co. in the 1930s and is added to vaccines only as a preservative—the theory being that multiple doses are taken from the same bottle and that thimerosal will protect against contamination. However, according to Geier, "the solution to any such problem is to make vaccines available in a single dose, which will cost the pharmaceuticals about one penny more. What is interesting is that if you look up the mumps, measles, rubella [MMR] vaccines in the PDR you'll see that they do not contain thimerosal because it would kill the live virus. The MMR is available in multidose packaging and, yet, there is no preservative—nothing. What they did was put a label on it that says 'This product does not contain preservatives. Handle with care.' It's that simple."

## Removing Mercury Would Reduce Autism

Geier insists, "I'm pro-vaccines, but the bottom line is that our kids are getting massive amounts of mercury. Mercury has been withdrawn from everything, including animal vaccines, yet we keep injecting it into our children. Everyone should absolutely refuse to take a vaccine shot that has thimerosal in it, and they should insist on reading the vaccine package insert. Our data showed that the more mercury children received in their childhood vaccines the more neurodevelopment disorders there are. We've looked at this every possible way and every time there's massive evidence to support it."

---

*Based on the Aventis [drug company] admission that the package insert does not reflect what is in the vaccine, it will be difficult to know when, if ever, the thimerosal actually has been removed.*

---

So, if everyone acknowledges the toxicity of mercury and top U.S. health officials have called for its removal, why is thimerosal still in vaccines? "Maybe," concludes Geier, "the mercury isn't being taken out all at once because if the pharmaceutical companies did that you would see an unbelievable change in the rate of autism and there would be massive lawsuits. If you look at the graphs now they go up and up. If you stop the thimerosal all at once you'd see the numbers fall dramatically."

Rep. Dan Burton (R-Ind.), a longtime advocate for victims of autism . . . explains that "thimerosal is a toxic substance—mercury—and should not be put in close proximity of people, should not be injected into people, especially children who have a newly formed immune system that may not be able to handle it. To my knowledge there never have been long-term tests on thimerosal and we never should have used mercury in vaccines, period. Now what we've got is an epidemic that is absolutely out of control."

The Indiana congressman continues, "One reason this isn't getting the attention it needs is that the Food and Drug Administration has very close ties to the pharmaceutical companies, as does the Department of Health and Human Services (HHS) and the Centers for Disease Control. I've said in the past that in some cases it appears that it's a revolving door and people leave government health agencies and go to work for the pharmaceuticals, which I think have undue influence on our health agencies. Of course, they may not want to look at this because there's a possibility that large claims would be filed and the pharmaceutical companies would have to cough up the money to take care of these kids who have been damaged." . . .

## Chronic Disease Replacing Infectious Disease

Barbara Loe Fisher is founder of the National Vaccine Information Center, a charitable organization dedicated to the prevention of vaccine injuries and deaths through public education. Fisher tells *Insight*, "There are many things in vaccines that could be causing these disorders, and thimerosal is only part of the problem. In the last 20 years, we've gone from giving children 23 doses of seven vaccines to 38 doses of 12 vaccines. I think the mercury is part of it for some kids, though I'm not sure it's the answer for all." But this is a no-brainer, says Fisher. "Mercury shouldn't be in vaccines. They've taken it out of everything else so why not the vaccines? The one thing that people really need to look at is the dramatic rise in chronic disease and disabilities in our kids in just the last two decades. You have to admit that there is something occurring that a growing number of children cannot get through without being immune-system and brain-system damaged. And what is the one thing that we expose every child to? Those vaccines."

Fisher concludes, "I've always argued that public health is not measured only by an absence of infectious disease. It also is measured by the absence of chronic disease. By that score we get a big fat 'F.' So we don't have measles and mumps, but look what we have now. It's just really simple: Take the mercury out and let's see what happens."

Even so, based on the Aventis admission that the package insert does not reflect what is in the vaccine, it will be difficult to know when, if ever, the thimerosal actually has been removed. This skews the data about the relationship between thimerosal and autism. More important, it means parents cannot be sure the vaccinations their children receive are free of mercury.

# Some Parents Feel They Must Lie to Avoid Vaccination of Their Children

*Steve LeBlanc*

*Steve LeBlanc is a reporter for the Associated Press news service.*

Sabrina Rahim doesn't practice any particular faith, but she had no problem signing a letter declaring that because of her deeply held religious beliefs, her 4-year-old son should be exempt from the vaccinations required to enter preschool.

She is among a small but growing number of parents around the country who are claiming religious exemptions to avoid vaccinating their children when the real reason may be skepticism of the shots or concern they can cause other illnesses. Some of these parents say they are being forced to lie because of the way the vaccination laws are written in their states.

"It's misleading," Rahim admitted, but she said she fears that earlier vaccinations may be to blame for her son's autism. "I find it very troubling, but for my son's safety, I feel this is the only option we have."

## Exemptions Increasing

An Associated Press [AP] examination of states' vaccination records and data from the Centers for Disease Control and Prevention [CDC] found that many states are seeing increases in the rate of religious exemptions claimed for kindergartners.

"Do I think that religious exemptions have become the default? Absolutely," said Dr. Paul Offit, head of infectious diseases at Children's Hospital in Philadelphia and one of the harshest critics of the anti-vaccine movement. He said the resistance to vaccines is "an irrational, fear-based decision."

Steve LeBlanc, "Parents Use Religion to Avoid Vaccines," abcnews.com, October 18, 2007. Reproduced by permission.

The number of exemptions is extremely small in percentage terms and represents just a few thousand of the 3.7 million children entering kindergarten in 2005, the most recent figure available.

But public health officials say it takes only a few people to cause an outbreak that can put large numbers of lives at risk. "When you choose not to get a vaccine, you're not just making a choice for yourself, you're making a choice for the person sitting next to you," said Dr. Lance Rodewald, director of the CDC's Immunization Services Division.

All states have some requirement that youngsters be immunized against such childhood diseases as measles, mumps, chickenpox, diphtheria and whooping cough.

Twenty-eight states, including Florida, Massachusetts and New York, allow parents to opt out for medical or religious reasons only. Twenty other states, among them California, Pennsylvania, Texas and Ohio, also allow parents to cite personal or philosophical reasons. Mississippi and West Virginia allow exemptions for medical reasons only.

From 2003 to 2007, religious exemptions for kindergartners increased, in some cases doubled or tripled, in 20 of the 28 states that allow only medical or religious exemptions, the AP found. Religious exemptions decreased in three of these states—Nebraska, Wyoming, South Carolina—and were unchanged in five others.

---

*While some parents ... have genuine religious objections to medicine, it is clear that others are simply distrustful of shots.*

---

The rate of exemption requests is also increasing. For example, in Massachusetts, the rate of those seeking exemptions has more than doubled in the past decade from 0.24 percent, or 210, in 1996 to 0.60 percent, or 474, in 2006.

In Florida, 1,249 children claimed religious exemptions in 2006, almost double the 661 who did so just four years earlier. That was an increase of 0.3 to 0.6 percent of the student population. Georgia, New Hampshire and Alabama saw their rates double in the past four years.

The numbers from the various states cannot be added up with accuracy. Some states used a sampling of students to gauge levels of vaccinations. Others surveyed all or nearly all students.

Fifteen of the 20 states that allow both religious and philosophical exemptions have seen increases in both, according to the AP's findings.

## Not All Religious Objections Genuine

While some parents, Christian Scientists and certain fundamentalists, for example, have genuine religious objections to medicine, it is clear that others are simply distrustful of shots.

Some parents say they are not convinced vaccinations help. Others fear the vaccinations themselves may make their children sick and even cause autism.

Even though government-funded studies have found no link between vaccines and autism, loosely organized groups of parents and even popular cultural figures such as radio host Don Imus have voiced concerns. Most of the furor on Internet message boards and Web sites has been about a mercury-based preservative once used in vaccines that some believe contributes to neurological disorders.

Unvaccinated children can spread diseases to others who have not gotten their shots or those for whom vaccinations provided less-than-complete protection.

In 1991, a religious group in Philadelphia that chose not to immunize its children touched off an outbreak of measles that claimed at least eight lives and sickened more than 700 people, mostly children.

And in 2005, an Indiana girl who had not been immunized picked up the measles virus at an orphanage in Romania and unknowingly brought it back to a church group. Within a month, the number of people infected had grown to 31 in what health officials said was the nation's worst outbreak of the disease in a decade.

Rachel Magni, a 35-year-old stay-at-home mother in Newton, Mass., said she is afraid vaccines could harm her children and "overwhelm their bodies." Even though she attends a Protestant church that allows vaccinations, Magni pursued a religious exemption so her 4-year-old daughter and 1-year-old son, who have never been vaccinated, could attend preschool. "I felt that the risk of the vaccine was worse than the risk of the actual disease," she said.

Barbara Loe Fisher, co-founder and president of the National Vaccine Information Center, one of the leading vaccine skeptic groups, said she discourages parents from pursuing religious exemptions unless they are genuine. Instead, Fisher said, parents should work to change the laws in their states. "We counsel that if you do not live in a state that has a philosophical exemption, you still have to obey the law," she said.

---

*A pediatrician ... said she counsels patients who worry that vaccines could harm their children to pursue a religious exemption if that is their only option.*

---

Even so, Fisher said, she empathizes with parents tempted to claim the religious exemption: "If a parent has a child who has had a deterioration after vaccination and the doctor says that's just a coincidence, you have to keep vaccinating this child, what is the parent left with?"

## Philosophical Exemptions

Offit said he knows of no state that enforces any penalty for parents who falsely claim a religious exemption.

"I think that wouldn't be worth it because that's just such an emotional issue for people. Our country was founded on the notion of religious freedom," he said.

In 2002, four Arkansas families challenged the state's policy allowing religious exemptions only if a parent could prove membership in a recognized religion prohibiting vaccination. The court struck down the policy and the state began allowing both religious and philosophical exemptions.

Religious and medical exemptions, which had been climbing, plummeted, while the number of philosophical exemptions spiked.

In the first year alone, more parents applied for philosophical exemptions than religious and medical exemptions combined. From 2001 to 2004, the total number of students seeking exemptions in Arkansas more than doubled, from 529 to 1,145.

Dr. Janet Levitan, a pediatrician in Brookline, Mass., said she counsels patients who worry that vaccines could harm their children to pursue a religious exemption if that is their only option.

"I tell them if you don't want to vaccinate for philosophical reasons and the state doesn't allow that, then say it's for religious reasons," she said. "It says you have to state that vaccination conflicts with your religious belief. It doesn't say you have to actually have that religious belief. So just state it."

# Many Scientific Studies of Vaccine Safety Are Flawed

*Robert F. Kennedy Jr.*

*Robert F. Kennedy Jr., the nephew of former U.S. president John F. Kennedy, is an attorney specializing in environmental issues and is the author of several books.*

The poisonous public attacks on Katie Wright [in June 2007]—for revealing that her autistic son Christian (grandson of NBC Chair Bob Wright) has recovered significant function after chelation treatments to remove mercury—surprised many observers unfamiliar with the acrimonious debate over the mercury-based vaccine preservative Thimerosal. But the patronizing attacks on the mothers of autistic children who have organized to oppose this brain-killing poison is one of the most persistent tactics employed by those defending Thimerosal against the barrage of scientific evidence linking it to the epidemic of pediatric neurological disorders, including autism. Mothers of autistics are routinely dismissed as irrational, hysterical, or, as a newspaper editor told me, "desperate to find the reason for their children's illnesses," and therefore, overwrought and disconnected.

But my experience with these women is inconsistent with those patronizing assessments. I've met or communicated with several hundred of these women. Instead of a desperate mob of irrational hysterics, I've found the anti-Thimerosal activists for the most part to be calm, grounded and extraordinarily patient. As a group, they are highly educated. Many of them are doctors, nurses, schoolteachers, pharmacists, psychologists, Ph.D.s and other professionals. Many of them approached the link skeptically and only through dispassionate and diligent investigation became convinced that Thimerosal-laced vac-

Robert F. Kennedy Jr., "Attack on Mothers," *Huffington Post*, June 19, 2007. Reproduced by permission.

cines destroyed their children's brains. As a group they have sat through hundreds of meetings and scientific conferences, and studied research papers and medical tests. They have networked with each other at meetings and on the Web. Along the way they have stoically endured the abuse routinely heaped upon them by the vaccine industry and public health authorities and casual dismissal by reporters and editors too lazy to do their jobs.

---

*Deliberately deceptive and fatally flawed studies were authored by vaccine industry consultants and paid for by Thimerosal producers.*

---

Many of these women tell a story virtually identical to Katie Wright's—I have now heard or seen this grim chronology recounted hundreds of times in conversations, e-mails and letters from mothers: At 2-1/2 years old, Christian Wright exceeded all milestones. He had 1,000 words, was toilet-trained, and enjoyed excellent social relations with his brother and others. Then his pediatrician gave him Thimerosal-laced vaccines. He cried all night, developed a fever and, over the coming months, this smart, healthy child disappeared. Christian lost the ability to speak, to interact with family members, to make eye contact or to point a finger. He is no longer toilet trained. He engaged in stereotypical behavior—screaming, head-banging, biting and uncontrolled aggression, and suffers continuously the agonizing pain of gastrointestinal inflammation.

## Disguising Thimerosal-Autism Link

After hearing that story a couple dozen times, a rational person might do some more investigation. That's when one encounters the overwhelming science—hundreds of research studies from dozens of countries showing the undeniable connection between mercury and Thimerosal and a wide range of neurological illnesses. In response to the overwhelming science, CDC [Centers for Disease Control and Prevention] and the pharmaceutical industry ginned up four European studies designed to disguise the link between autism and Thimerosal. Their purpose was to provide plausible deniability for the consequences of their awful decision to allow brain-killing mercury to be injected into our youngest children. Those deliberately deceptive and fatally flawed studies were authored by vaccine industry consultants and paid for by Thimerosal producers and published largely in compromised journals that neglected to disclose the myriad conflicts of their authors in violation of standard peer-review ethics. As I've shown elsewhere, these studies were borderline fraud, using statistical deceptions to mislead the public and regulatory community.

The CDC and IOM [National Academy of Sciences Institute of Medicine] base their defense of Thimerosal on these flimsy studies, their own formidable reputations, and their faith that journalists won't take the time to critically read the science. The bureaucrats are simultaneously using their influence, energies and clout to derail, defund and suppress any scientific study that may verify the link between Thimerosal and brain disorders. (These would include epidemiological studies comparing the records of vaccinated children with those of unvaccinated populations like the Amish or homeschooled kids who appear to enjoy dramatically reduced levels of autism and other neurological disorders.) The federal agencies have refused to release the massive public health information accumulated in their Vaccine Safety Database (VSD) apparently to keep independent scientists from reviewing evidence that could prove the link. They are also muzzling or blackballing scientists who want to conduct such studies.

Ironically, it is the same voices that once blamed autism on "bad parenting," and "uninvolved" moms that are now faulting these mothers for being too involved.

Due to this campaign of obfuscation and public deception, Thimerosal-based vaccines continue to sicken millions of children around the world and potential treatments—like the chelation that benefited Christian Wright—are kept out of the hands of the mainstream doctors now treating autistic kids with less effective tools. Like thousands of other mothers of autistic children, Katie Wright knows what sickened her child. Her efforts to spare other families this catastrophe, deployed with a cool head and calm demeanor, are truly heroic. Maybe it's time we all started listening. Maybe it's time to start respecting and honoring the maternal instincts and hard work of Katie and her fellow mothers by aggressively funding the studies that might verify or dispute them.

# The Cervical Cancer Vaccine Has Not Been Proven Safe or Effective

*Cathy Gulli, Lianne George, and John Intini*

*Cathy Gulli, Lianne George, and John Intini are staff writers for the Canadian magazine* Maclean's.

The morning after Emily Cunningham got a shot of Gardasil, the new vaccine that protects against four strains of the human papilloma virus (HPV) that can cause cervical cancer and genital warts, she woke up with a headache, and neck and back pain. By 9 p.m. that evening in April, she had a fever so high "you could feel the heat rising from her a foot away," according to her mother, Laurie. She was delirious during the night, and the following day couldn't walk without assistance. Bedridden for nearly a week, the 18-year-old from Wyoming missed school, and took Tylenol every four hours. "If Emily had been the only one to get sick we would have said she must have had something else [like the flu]," explained Laurie, "but we know of three other students to have reactions, that is why we are concerned."

Emily's story is only one of 1,637 complaints involving Gardasil, filed as of May [2007] to the Vaccine Adverse Event Reporting System (VAERS), a national surveillance database sponsored by the Food and Drug Administration (FDA) and the Centers for Disease Control and Prevention (CDC) in the United States. One could discount what happened to Emily because she had a flu shot that same day, but other really bad reactions have been reported, including seizures, paralysis—and worst of all, three deaths, including one girl who "died of a blood clot three hours after getting the Gardasil vaccine," reads one complaint. Elsewhere in the world there have been reports of similar reactions. In Melbourne, Australia, where a national HPV vaccination program started in April [2007], 26 girls reportedly fainted and were mildly paralyzed after getting one shot each.

## Medical Evidence Lacking

In almost every instance, the response of medical authorities and government officials is the same: bad reactions are rare. When they do occur, there's no evidence that Gardasil was the cause. Arguably, both points could be true. Some say the problem, however, is that no one really knows, medically speaking, just how dangerous this vaccine could be. "Usually at this stage in the life span of a vaccine we would not have this kind of action." *Maclean's* has heard from Abby Lippman, an epidemiologist at McGill University who recently aired her concerns about the speed with which Gardasil has been adopted in the *Canadian Medical Association Journal*. "We're making guesses that it's going to last long, that [we're immunizing] the right age [of girls], and that it's effective. We don't have a solid basis for this thought." . . .

While everyone debates the moral and political consequences of endorsing Gardasil, the fundamental, essential medical and scientific debate remains untouched. So, in a few weeks, when thousands of girls concerned about Facebook and who will be in their class this year—not HPV—go back to school, many will become part of the biggest Canadian science experiment in decades. They will be the guinea pigs.

To find out the worst case scenario when it comes to Gardasil, one need only hear the stories of parents whose children have become ill or died after receiving the vaccine. Recently, one angry father from Chicago phoned up John Driscoll, an attorney at the law firm Brown & Crouppen in St. Louis, Mo. Shortly after receiving Gardasil, his daughter was diagnosed with Guillain-Barré syndrome, an autoimmune disease. It starts with tingling sensations in the legs, which then travel to the upper body, and finally become so intense in the muscles they paralyze, though often they diminish over time. "He believes it was linked," says Driscoll, and wants to sue Merck & Co., Inc., the U.S. pharmaceutical company that manufactures Gardasil. This will be the first such lawsuit, but Driscoll, who believes the vaccine was rushed to market, predicts that, "unfortunately, we'll get more and more calls about this in the future."

In fact, Guillain-Barré syndrome is one of the more serious adverse reactions noted in the hundreds of complaints filed to VAERS. "When you go to your doctor's office, the list of symptoms is very short: dizziness, fainting. But there's a whole laundry list of potentially serious side effects," says Dee Grothe, an investigator at the Washington-based watchdog organization Judicial Watch, which filed freedom of information requests to access details about negative reactions relating to Gardasil. "This is information that everybody receiving the shot should know," she says.

---

*Many believe there is still not enough known about the HPV vaccine to warrant mass inoculation.*

---

Merck Frosst Canada Ltd., which is the Canadian manufacturer of the vaccine, sees no proof that Gardasil is responsible for the illnesses or deaths. "There is a relationship between Gardasil and these events, but there's no cause and effect," says Sheila Murphy, manager of public affairs for Merck Frosst. Similarly, the FDA and CDC have said there's no likely connection (they claim the two deaths from blood clots were caused by birth control pills taken at the time of immunization, and the third death was due to heart inflammation brought on by the flu). But some skeptics find these explanations ambiguous and suspicious. "I'm not a doctor, but when

I read this information, to me, that is a clear indication that there may have been a problem," says Grothe.

## Long-Term Effects Unknown

It's obvious that even in the best-case scenario, many believe there is still not enough known about the HPV vaccine to warrant mass inoculation programs. For starters, there are concerns that not enough nine- to 15-year-old girls were studied during clinical trials for Gardasil. Approximately 1,200 were enrolled, and according to a report by the Canadian Women's Health Network [CWHN], only 100 of them were age nine, and that limited group was only followed for 18 months. "Clearly, this is a very weak information base on which to construct a policy of mass vaccinations for all girls aged nine to 13, as per the National Advisory Committee on Immunization's recommendations," the CWHN report summarized.

The CWHN also worries about the long-term effectiveness of Gardasil, given the longest that clinical trial participants who received the vaccine were tracked was for five years. "If we're talking about vaccinating nine-year-old girls we want protection for 20 or 30 years," concedes Laura Koutsky, an epidemiologist at the University of Washington who helped Merck design the clinical trials and oversaw them for Gardasil. "Can we infer protection out to that period? We don't know. But we have evidence that suggests it's likely."

Inference, though, is not the scientific evidence some expect. Analysis beyond clinical trials is critical to ensuring public safety, warns Lippman. "What happens in the real world can be very different from what happens in the clinical research world," where girls are in a controlled environment, and get health examinations frequently to gauge any problems. "The real world is where we find out what really happens when you let a vaccine loose on a population."

A study in the May [2007] issue of the *New England Journal of Medicine* speaks to how real world situations such as "imperfect compliance" (such as not receiving all three doses of Gardasil), and a girl's previous exposure to HPV, could take Gardasil's 70 per cent protection against precancerous lesions (which lead to cervical cancer) down to a staggering 17 per cent. "That's one more reason we should be slowing down," says Hans Krueger, a health care consultant who has advised the [British Columbia] Cancer Agency, among other organizations, on Gardasil. "This suggests to me we just don't know enough." . . .

Canada's widespread adoption of the HPV vaccine in some ways makes the country a guinea pig for Gardasil on an international scale, says Diane M. Harper, a lead researcher in the development of the HPV vaccine, and a professor at Dartmouth Medical School in New Hampshire who has worked with Merck and GSK [GlaxoSmithKline]. While developing nations where cervical cancer rates are high could stand to benefit the most from Gardasil, they aren't "going to readily adopt a vaccine unless they feel comfortable that other countries have adopted the vaccine and done well and seen success with it. That's the history of how the world has gone in health care."

---

*Hype around Gardasil has created a false sense of urgency about the need for the vaccine.*

---

Merck has explicitly stated that Gardasil does not offer total protection against cervical cancer. And so the question remains, in the absence of HPV 16 and 18 [two strains of cervical cancer that Gardasil protects against], what's to stop other resistant strains of the virus from evolving into something more aggressive? "We're making educated guesses of what we think will happen to the virus in the future based on what we know of the virus right now," says Koutsky. A super-strain of

HPV is unlikely to occur, she continues, because the papilloma genome does not evolve at a rapid pace. "But it's true we don't know," she says.

One possibility is that other strains, which cause the remaining 30 per cent of cervical cancers, may become more prevalent. "If you knock off two big tough drug dealers who control 70 per cent of the market and take them to jail, the other guys will quickly fill the void," says Andrew Lynk, a Sydney, [Nova Scotia]–based pediatrician. "We've seen that also in the vaccination world."

In the report published by the Canadian Women's Health Network, medical experts point to a cautionary tale in Alaska, where native children were inoculated en masse against a strain of pneumococcal pneumonia. A follow-up study found that, since the vaccinations in 2004, "the invasive pneumococcal disease rate caused by non-vaccine serotypes [had] increased 140 per cent compared with the pre-vaccine period." Studies like this one, the CWHN warns, demand that the medical community, the government and the public consider "how Gardasil, or any other HPV vaccine, might alter the natural history of HPV infections—and whether other HPV strains might move in to occupy the vacated niche—before engaging in a massive vaccination program." . . .

## Low Risk of Developing Cancer

The HPV vaccine has been sold by Merck and its proponents as a tool for ending cervical cancer. But a quick look at statistics shows that the risk of developing this disease, let alone dying from it, is very low. . . . But hype around Gardasil has created a false sense of urgency about the need for the vaccine, according to cautious observers such as Lippman. "If there was an epidemic and people were dropping dead on the street corner, you'd want to do something," she says. But "we have the luxury to reflect, think and act wisely. Then we can put our foot into the street and cross. [Right now] I'm in the yellow light mode."

When HPV strains, of which there are up to 200, do cause infections, they are usually slow to grow, which makes identifying them through Pap smears relatively easy. . . .

Despite these promising outcomes, cervical cancer is being turned into a new millennium polio, according to Dr. Sharon Moalem, author of *Survival of the Sickest*, and a neurogeneticist and evolutionary biologist at New York's Mount Sinai School of Medicine. "The problem that I've seen is many of the advocates for [Gardasil] say everyone should be vaccinated, but this is not polio and a lot of people can have HPV and not every variant of HPV causes cancer as far as we know."

In fact, most people will wind up with HPV at some point in their lives and fight it off without ever even knowing they were exposed to the virus, which is primarily transmitted through skin contact with genitalia. According to the Canadian Women's Health Network, most women who don't smoke, eat well and have a healthy immune system will clear the virus without any treatment. And the Public Health Agency of Canada has said that more than 80 per cent of HPV infections acquired at an early age were gone within a year and a half. Even better, after a woman has fought off a strain, she has almost no chance of contracting it again.

HPV is so common that even infants and children have been found with infections, suggesting that the virus isn't just transmitted sexually, says Krueger. While there is no conclusive literature explaining how else it might be contracted, some have suggested that newborns could acquire HPV while in their mother's vaginal tract. However it happens, Gardasil critics point to these puzzling cases as another reason why the vaccine—which is only preventive, and won't have any effect on those who already have HPV—shouldn't be given to all girls. "These data do warn against assuming too quickly the lack of exposure to HPV in even young girls in developing vaccination programs and policies," states the CWHN.

Even for the limited number of women who do wind up contracting the HPV strains that could lead to cervical cancer, some say current screening methods—Pap smears—are effective and safe ways of preventing the disease. About 79 per cent of Canadian women between the ages of 18 and 69 have had a Pap in the last three years, and according to the immunization advisory committee, this has "led to dramatic reductions in invasive cancer in the developed world."

Further proof of the test's effectiveness is found in the fact that the majority of women who do wind up with cervical cancer—60 per cent—were either unscreened or underscreened, meaning they didn't get their Pap at all, or didn't get it on schedule. . . .

## Vaccine Will Not End Cervical Cancer

Even if HPV vaccination programs continue to expand, the public needs to understand that young women can still develop HPV infection and cervical cancer after being immunized, say experts. Paps will be a critical complement to Gardasil, insists the immunization advisory committee. "Women who have been vaccinated will still be susceptible to other [high-risk] HPV types. Even if those types are less prevalent than HPV 16 or 18, these women should still expect to take part in the currently recommended cervical cancer screening programs."

Harper, the HPV researcher at Dartmouth, tells of a yet unpublished study showing that, even if every female aged 12 to 26 is vaccinated, if they don't go for Pap tests thereafter the rate of cervical cancer will actually go up compared to pre-immunization rates. "So there is significant danger in people feeling this vaccine offers them a force field protection," says Harper, "and that could actually rebound back to us because there are other HPV types out there and they're not going to stop causing cancer just because we've given a vaccine."

All these questions and caveats highlight just how little medical and scientific evidence exists to make the case against mass inoculation a no-brainer. "The medical, scientific community has to sit down and say, what are really the costs and benefits here?" says Moalem. "It's been turned into a public health issue and everyone's trying to spin it their own way and most cancer doctors will tell parents, why would you risk having your child get cervical cancer if I can give you a vaccine to prevent it? But they don't know what the long-term costs are."

Her strong recommendation is for parents to talk to their children about HPV as a sexually transmitted virus, and its link to cervical cancer, among other illnesses. "It's much easier as a parent to get your child to have a vaccine than to sit down and have a conversation and say, using condoms can reduce HPV exposure, therefore that reduces cervical cancer. I'll just give you a shot, then we don't have to talk about it," she says. Moalem believes the original marketing of Gardasil as the vaccine against cervical cancer has been misleading. "That's not what this is. This is a vaccine against a sexually transmitted disease. I think that's what people should be very clear on. That really would change the frame of the debate."

Until more medical and scientific analysis illuminates just what Gardasil will do to young girls, Krueger is wary. "We have a virus here that has so many different types and affects so many body systems that it's just very complex. The fact that we have a vaccine against HPV types that cause cervical cancer is a medical breakthrough," he says, but then adds, "My girls will not be vaccinated. That's not just because of deaths or adverse effects, it's because of all these unknowns."

# The Benefits of Vaccines Far Outweigh the Risks

*Aubrey Noelle Stimola*

*Aubrey Noelle Stimola is assistant director of public health at the American Council on Science and Health.*

According to the Centers for Disease Control and Prevention (CDC), rubella, a virus notorious for causing birth defects, stillbirths, and miscarriages, has been eliminated from the United States. During its last major U.S. outbreak in the mid-60s, there were 12.5 million cases of rubella, resulting in 20,000 cases of congenital rubella syndrome, 11,600 babies born deaf, 11,250 fetal deaths, 2,100 newborn deaths, 3,580 babies born blind, and 1,800 more mentally handicapped. As a direct result of the nation's successful immunization program, incidence was down to only nine cases [in 2004]—none of which originated domestically.

The announcement comes as a welcome reminder of the benefits bestowed by vaccines at a time when media coverage has audiences wondering if vaccines should be viewed skeptically. Is the announcement reason to celebrate? Indeed. Is it reason enough to forgo your child's rubella inoculation—or your own? Absolutely not.

Beginning with the work of Edward Jenner over 200 years ago, vaccines are the cause of decreased morbidity and mortality rates for fourteen infectious diseases, including smallpox, pertussis, diphtheria, and polio; are a promising candidate for mounting a defense against HIV, the virus that causes AIDS; and may one day be used to target cancer cells. Recently, however, scientifically unsubstantiated media and activ-

Aubrey Noelle Stimola, "Vaccination Still Wise Despite Domestic Eradication of Rubella," *American Council on Science and Health*, March 30, 2005. Reproduced with permission of American Council on Science and Health (ACSH). For more information on ACSH visit www.ACSH.org.

ist reports about vaccine safety have resulted in parental confusion over how to best protect children's health. On one hand, parents are urged by pediatricians to inoculate their children against the wide range of potentially deadly but vaccine-preventable diseases. On the other, they are buffeted by alarmist reports that the documented rise in the number of autism spectrum disorder diagnoses and other developmental delays could be attributable to the recommended pediatric immunization schedule.

Despite the fact that the large majority of data do not support such a link, media-perpetuated skepticism has led more and more parents to opt out of having their children vaccinated. This dangerous trend is compounded by the fact that—due to the success of the immunization program—younger generations of parents don't remember the widespread suffering caused by diseases such as polio, which often left surviving children confined to wheelchairs, crutches, or iron lungs.

## A Resurgence of Diseases

If parents interpret announcements like the one made recently by the CDC as indicators that it is safe to opt out of having their children fully vaccinated—particularly if they have also been led to believe that in so doing they are protecting their children from becoming autistic—it is plausible that the U.S. could experience a resurgence of diseases that have been drastically or entirely curbed domestically but are still endemic in other parts of the world. Such is the case with pertussis, more commonly known as whooping cough. Once on the decline in the U.S., the incidence of this potentially deadly disease has risen steadily in recent decades—from 1,010 cases in 1976 to 8,296 in 2002—primarily as a result of waning immunity in adults, who then transmit the disease to the increasing population of unvaccinated children.

For this reason, health officials have reinforced the recommendation that pertussis vaccine be given to all children, and research is being done regarding the risk/benefit ratio of providing boosters to adolescents and adults.

Similarly, because elimination of rubella within the U.S. is not equivalent to total global eradication, as CDC director Julie Gerberding points out, "we are at constant risk for reintroduction of the virus from other parts of the world." For that reason, she continues, "we cannot afford to relax our emphasis on immunization now." The CDC has stated that children should continue to be immunized against rubella, since global eradication of the virus is "a long way off."

---

*Parents should heed the advice of pediatricians and make sure their children continue to be properly immunized.*

---

For another example, we need only look at the poliovirus, for which a vaccine was developed by Jonas Salk fifty years ago. Even though the disease was declared eliminated in the U.S. in 1979 and in the Western hemisphere in 1991, the polio vaccine is still part of the recommended pediatric vaccines schedule due to its continued existence in other parts of the world, such as Africa, where 1,263 documented cases occurred in 2004. In this time of frequent and convenient world travel, it is plausible that poliovirus, which in its most devastating form can cause muscle paralysis and death, could be brought back to the U.S. Given the possibility of resurgence, the vaccine will be given until the virus is eradicated globally.

Smallpox, on the other hand, is an example of a vaccine-preventable disease that was not only eliminated from the U.S. but also eradicated worldwide. The last naturally occurring case in the world was in Somalia in 1977, though the virus exists in a few research laboratories. Once routinely administered (just ask people born before 1972 to show you their scars), the smallpox vaccine has not been part of the immunization schedule for over thirty years, as the risk of resurgence is extremely low, far lower than that of rubella. Unlike the vaccines mentioned above, smallpox vaccine also has significant risk of adverse effects, a factor that must be taken into careful consideration if smallpox ever sees a resurgence.

To summarize, while we should certainly celebrate the success of the national immunization program in eliminating the domestic incidence of rubella, it and similar successes need to be viewed in context. Given that the risk of contracting rubella still exists and that the risk associated with receiving the vaccine—as long as one is not pregnant—is far less, parents should heed the advice of pediatricians and make sure their children continue to be properly immunized.

## Non-Medical Exemptions on the Rise

Fear of harm is the most common reason given by parents who choose not to have their children vaccinated against preventable diseases, according to an article in the May [2005] issue of the *Archives of Pediatrics and Adolescent Medicine*.

---

*Lost amidst the pervasive paranoia is the irrefutable scientific fact that vaccines have saved millions of lives worldwide.*

---

Over the last decade, the number of parents taking advantage of "non-medical exemption" from pediatric vaccination requirements has been steadily on the rise in several states. Such a trend greatly increases these children's risk of contracting potentially deadly but vaccine-preventable illnesses that they can then pass on to younger children who are too young to be vaccinated, as well as individuals who cannot be vaccinated for medical reasons. Further, these susceptible children tend to be geographically clustered, which greatly increases the likelihood of disease outbreaks due to a loss of "community" or "herd" immunity, a crucial factor in the overall success of immunization programs.

A survey designed to determine the motivations of parents claiming non-medical exemptions for their children showed that 69% of the parents of 277 unvaccinated children in four states claimed exemption over concern that vaccines cause harm, presumably more harm than good. Compared to the parents of vaccinated children, these parents were also found to have a low perception of their children's susceptibility to vaccine preventable illnesses and a poor understanding of the danger posed by these diseases.

The overwhelming effectiveness of the immunization program, a health intervention that has been credited with a substantial portion of the increase in life expectancy over the past century, makes skepticism about vaccine safety and effectiveness seem misplaced. Successes of immunization include the worldwide eradication of smallpox, the elimination of polio in the Western hemisphere, the recent domestic eradication of rubella, and substantial decreases in cases of measles, mumps, tetanus, diphtheria, and *Haemophilus Influenza type b* (Hib) worldwide. The paradox of this tremendous public health success—as explained by Dr. Bruce Gellin and colleagues in the journal *Pediatrics*—is that, because vaccines have curtailed so many diseases, "the diseases that vaccines prevent no longer serve as a reminder of the need for vaccination." In other words, how many people born today understand the crippling effects of polio? The congenital deformities caused by rubella? The slow suffocation that can result from diphtheria? As Dr. David Salisbury, Principal Medical Officer for the UK [United Kingdom] Health Department states, "If parents have fear of disease but no fear of vaccines, the argument in favor of vaccines is clearcut. If they have no fear of disease but also no fear of vaccines, there may be inertia. When they have no fear of disease, but fear of vaccines, parents are likely to refuse immunization." Indeed, there is an easily recognized and ironic pattern here: as disease incidence goes down, vaccine skepticism goes up.

Currently, concerns about vaccines, even those without scientific merit, carry tremendous weight in the eyes of a public fearful of government conspiracy and big-business dishonesty. This is particularly true in light of recent drug recalls, daily health scares, and increasingly antagonistic debates over healthcare and scientific research. Lost amidst the pervasive paranoia is the irrefutable scientific fact that vaccines have saved millions of lives worldwide.

Are vaccines entirely risk-free? Nothing is. Failure to take action based on the existence of *some risk* is to rely on the dubious precautionary principle [the idea that it is better to be safe than sorry]. The crucial question is whether the benefits of vaccines vastly outweigh the risks associated with a failure to use vaccines. Indeed they do. Already, we are seeing a resurgence of pertussis in the U.S., due in part to waning adult immunity and the transmission of the disease from infected adults to unvaccinated children. This is the message that must find its way back into headlines—before vaccine-preventable diseases make a devastating comeback.

# Giving Multiple Vaccines to Children Is Safe

## Centers for Disease Control and Prevention

*Centers for Disease Control and Prevention (CDC) compose the principal U.S. government public health agency.*

H*ow many vaccines does CDC recommend for children?* Currently, CDC recommends vaccination against 14 vaccine-preventable diseases. Because some of these vaccines have to be administered more than once, a child may receive up to 23 shots by the time he or she is 2 years of age. Depending on the timing, a child might receive up to six shots during one visit to the doctor.

*Why does CDC recommend that children receive so many shots?* CDC recommends vaccination to protect children against 14 diseases, including measles, mumps, rubella (German measles), varicella (chickenpox), hepatitis B, diphtheria, tetanus, pertussis (whooping cough), Haemophilus influenza type B (Hib), polio, influenza (flu), and pneumococcal disease. Vaccines are our best defense against these diseases, which often result in serious complications such as pneumonia, meningitis (swelling of the lining of the brain), liver cancer, bloodstream infections, and even death.

*Why are these vaccines given at such a young age? Wouldn't it be safer to wait?* Children are given vaccines at a young age because this is when they are most vulnerable to certain diseases. Newborn babies are immune to some diseases because they have antibodies given to them from their mothers. However, this immunity only lasts about a year. Further, most young children do not have maternal immunity to diphtheria,

Centers for Disease Control and Prevention, "Frequently Asked Questions About Multiple Vaccines and the Immune System," October 31, 2007.

whooping cough, polio, tetanus, hepatitis B, or Hib. If a child is not vaccinated and is exposed to a disease germ, the child's body may not be strong enough to fight the disease.

An infant's immune system is more than ready to respond to the very small number of weakened and killed antigens in vaccines. Babies have the capacity to respond to foreign antigens even before they are born. The human immune system has evolved since organisms began living on Earth and represents a culmination of the "best" of this experience. Just as babies are born with a full-length digestive system that simply stretches as the baby grows, they also are born with a well developed immune system that can produce a variety of needed antibodies. However, infants lack the memory cells trained to defend against specific diseases. Because of this, they are particularly susceptible to diseases such as diphtheria, whooping cough, polio, tetanus, hepatitis B, and Hib. This is an important reason why the recommended childhood vaccination schedule begins so early—to prevent the diseases that children are susceptible to at such a young age.

*I've heard people talk about "simultaneous" and "combination" vaccines. What does this mean? Why are vaccines administered this way?* "Simultaneous vaccination" is when multiple vaccines are administered during the same doctor's visit, usually in separate limbs (e.g., one in each arm). A "combination vaccine" consists of two or more separate vaccines that have been combined into a single shot. Combination vaccines have been in use in the United States since the mid-1940s. Examples of combination vaccines in current use are: DTaP (diphtheria-tetanus-pertussis), trivalent IPV (three strains of inactivated polio vaccine), MMR (measles-mumps-rubella), DTaP-Hib, and Hib-HepB (hepatitis B).

Giving a child several vaccinations during the same visit offers two practical advantages. First, we want to immunize children as quickly as possible to give them protection during the vulnerable early months of their lives. Second, giving, several vaccinations at the same time means fewer office visits, which saves parents both time and money and may be less traumatic for the child.

---

*No evidence suggests that the recommended childhood vaccines can "overload" the immune system.*

---

*Is simultaneous vaccination with multiple vaccines safe? Wouldn't it be safer to separate combination vaccines and spread them out, vaccinating against just one disease at a time?* The available scientific data show that simultaneous vaccination with multiple vaccines has no adverse effect on the normal childhood immune system. A number of studies have been conducted to examine the effects of giving various combinations of vaccines simultaneously. These studies have shown that the recommended vaccines are as effective in combination as they are individually, and that such combinations carry no greater risk for adverse side effects. Consequently, both the Advisory Committee on Immunization Practices and the American Academy of Pediatrics recommend simultaneous administration of all routine childhood vaccines when appropriate. Research is underway to find methods to combine more antigens in a single vaccine injection (for example, MMR and chickenpox). This will provide all the advantages of the individual vaccines, but will require fewer shots.

Another advantage is that combination vaccines result in fewer shots and less discomfort for children. In addition, spreading out the administration of separate vaccines may leave children unnecessarily vulnerable to disease.

*Can so many vaccines, given so early in life, overwhelm a child's immune system, suppressing it so it does not function correctly?* No evidence suggests that the recommended childhood vaccines can "overload" the immune system. In contrast, from the moment babies are born, they are exposed to numerous bacteria and viruses on a daily basis. Eating food introduces new bacteria into the body; numerous bacteria live in the mouth and nose; and an infant places his or her hands or other objects in his or her mouth hundreds of times every hour, exposing the immune system to still more antigens. An upper respiratory viral infection exposes a child to 4 to 10 antigens, and a case of "strep throat" to 25 to 50.

*Adverse Events Associated with Childhood Vaccines*, a 1994 report from the Institute of Medicine, states: "In the face of these normal events, it seems unlikely that the number of separate antigens contained in childhood vaccines . . . would represent an appreciable added burden on the immune system that would be immunosuppressive."

# Anti-Vaccine Fanatics Are Free Riders

*Michael Fumento*

*Michael Fumento is a senior fellow at the Hudson Institute in Washington, D.C., and a nationally syndicated columnist for Scripps Howard News Service.*

Grant the anti–childhood vaccine fanatics this, they are dogged. No amount of data, no number of studies from any array of sources will sway them from their assertions that thimerosal, a mercury-containing vaccine preservative once used in many such injections, is causing the so-called "autism epidemic."

A devastating California Department of Public Health study in the current *Archives of General Psychiatry* hasn't swayed them either. Lynne Redwood, co-founder of one anti-vaccine website, warned the *Baltimore Sun*, "Our children are still getting exposed to mercury." She cautioned against "clos-[ing] the books on thimerosal," even though the study has slammed them shut.

## Anti-Vaccine Activists Are Fanatical

But, for the rest of us there are two valuable lessons here. First, the lack of a thimerosal connection to the developmental disorder has once again been proved. Second, anti-vaccine activists are truly fanatical. As a *British Medical Journal* book reviewer rightly said, they live in an "angry and paranoid universe."

Anti-vaccinators like Redwood operate over 150 websites. Many of these sites claim not only a thimerosal-vaccine connection but a Massive World Wide Conspiracy to cover up the alleged link. The paranoiacs have sent death threats to Public Health Service officials who subsequently quit their jobs in fear.

In the face of such fears, thimerosal was removed from all childhood vaccines as of March 2001 (except flu shots, which contain a trace amount). This allowed a before and after comparison. The angry paranoids and those who make a living catering to them confidently declared that soon the data would show a dramatic drop in diagnoses.

Indeed they quickly asserted that the data *had* done so, as did former *New York Times* writer David Kirby, author of the influential 2005 book *Evidence of Harm—Mercury in Vaccines and the Autism Epidemic: A Medical Controversy.*

Never mind that this alleged peak, in 2002, came far too early to have reflected cessation of thimerosal use.

Later the father-son team of Drs. Mark and David Geier published a study they claimed showed a dramatic 35 percent drop, also beginning in 2002.

The Geiers make their living as expert witnesses and consultants for lawyers making vaccine harm claims against the government's National Vaccine Injury Compensation Program. Big surprise.

## Bad News for Fearmongers

Now that there has been enough time for serious study, the news is good for parents and bad for the fearmongers. The *Archives* study evaluated autistic children referred to the state's Developmental Services System and covered the years 1995 to March of 2007. Children as young as age 3 were evaluated. If thimerosal-preserved vaccines cause autism, the researchers said, diagnoses should have started falling in 2004—not 2002.

But there has been no plummet, no decline, no leveling. There hasn't been the least bit of decrease in the increasing number of cases of autism.

"We are reassured that we found no link between routine childhood vaccination and increases in childhood autism in the data," study lead author and California DPH [Department of Public Health] Medical Officer Robert Schechter, a physician, told the medical e-zine *WebMD*.

Nor are these findings anomalous. As the *Archives* paper noted, "Our findings are in concordance with the rigorous 2004 review of at least 12 previous published and unpublished studies by the IOM [Institute of Medicine] Immunization Safety Committee, which concluded that the body of evidence rejected a causal relationship between [thimerosal-containing vaccines] and autism."

---

*The driving force against sound medicine remains that angry paranoid universe that effectively opposes all vaccinations.*

---

Included in the IOM review were three studies looking at the entire populations of Sweden, Denmark, and Canada. In all three countries thimerosal-containing vaccines were discontinued in the late 1990s and in all three, as with California, autism rates climbed at the same pace as before.

## Some Anti-Vaccinationists Are Opportunists

None of which has done the least to dampen the ardor or arrogance of the anti-vaccinationists, who in fairness aren't all nuts. Some of them are just opportunists.

Included in the opportunistic category are environmentalists such as the Environmental Working Group and individuals like environmental crusader Robert F. Kennedy Jr. Scaring parents over thimerosal in vaccines is intended to buttress their campaign against coal-fired power plants.

The farcical relationship here is that thimerosal comprises about 50 percent ethyl mercury, while the stuff from power plants that gets into fish that pregnant women are warned about eating is called methyl mercury.

Despite the difference of merely one letter (you know, like "cat" and "rat"), scientists say there is a drastic difference in how each is metabolized and thus their potential for harm. That said, the Maternal Nutrition Group, a coalition of nutrition groups and experts, including several federal agencies, concluded a review of studies by recommending that pregnant women eat far more fatty fish than they do, citing in part a low risk even from methyl mercury.

But the driving force against sound medicine remains that angry paranoid universe that effectively opposes all vaccinations. Critics also fiercely target the MMR vaccine (measles-mumps-rubella), insisting it, too, causes autism—though MMR *never* contained thimerosal.

---

*If enough people free ride, then herd immunity is lost and what follows is the return of childhood diseases we hardly think about anymore.*

---

The most recent "expert" to weigh in on that is former *Playboy* Playmate Jenny McCarthy, who demonstrated her 38-C IQ in claims on Oprah [Winfrey's talk show] and in her best-selling book. She's part of the bizarre segment of our society that sees childhood vaccines as some sort of black magic and have latched onto the unquestionable rise in autism rates to make the point.

Indeed, the single group most affiliated with this branch of thinking, that published the Geier paper in its online journal, is the Association of American Physicians and Surgeons, Inc. It has its roots in the old anti-fluoridation far right which really did consider fluoridation a Communist plot.

Yet the evidence has long pointed to genetics as being the overwhelming causation factor in autism, evidence strengthened by three studies published in the January 10 [2008] *American Journal of Human Genetics.*

As to the indisputably large increase in autism diagnoses, the so-called "autism epidemic," "diagnoses" appears to be the key word. Over the years, the definition of the disorder has been expanded. The increase in autism diagnoses in kids has paralleled a decrease in mental retardation diagnoses. Growing awareness of the problem has also led to identification and labeling of cases that once were missed.

One shouldn't have to add that increased identification and proper diagnosis of a problem is a *good* thing.

## Anti-Vaccinationists Are Free Riders

Anti-vaccine advocates have scared parents throughout not only the U.S. but many other countries into refusing to vaccinate their children. These parents become free riders, relying on those parents who do vaccinate to keep diseases at bay through "herd immunity." That means that immunization rates in the wider population are high enough (for example, 85 percent for diphtheria) to protect those not immunized.

But if enough people free ride, then herd immunity is lost and what follows is the return of childhood diseases we hardly think about anymore. Diseases like pertussis have made comebacks in countries as diverse as the U.K. [United Kingdom], the U.S., Australia, Japan, and Sweden after vaccination scares. Better known as "whooping cough," pertussis is a highly contagious bacterial disease that causes uncontrollable, violent coughing. Pertussis cases went from fewer than 8,000 in the U.S. in 2001 to over 25,000 in 2005.

Vaccine fearmongers won't acknowledge any of this. Many even claim vaccines never brought these diseases under control in the first place and therefore play no role in keeping them in check.

Appealing to such people is impossible, but the damage can be limited by appeals to those susceptible to their vicious and false propaganda. The Public Health Service needs to start a public interest campaign to fight back. If only they could find a spokesperson with a 39-D IQ....

# CHAPTER 2

# Should Routine Vaccinations Be Mandatory?

# Overview: Vaccination Controversy Centers on the Right to Choose

*Logan Molyneux*

*Logan Molyneux is a reporter for the* Provo Daily Herald *in Utah.*

Marie Hansen of Spanish Fork [Utah] says something changed the day she took her son Dylan to his 1-year-old doctor's appointment.

Until then, Dylan had been successfully overcoming developmental problems caused by his low birth weight. But when he got his MMR and chicken pox immunization shots, he started crying uncontrollably and stopped breathing regularly. Doctors and nurses were eventually able to stabilize him, but Hansen says she never learned exactly what happened. She assumes it was a seizure, but all she really knows is that she soon realized something was wrong.

"He just seemed really off the next week," Hansen said. "He didn't really run a fever or anything, he was just off. The best way I can describe it is that he kind of lost the spark in his eye. I can show you pictures and it's just night and day."

Hansen is among a small but growing number of parents who choose not to vaccinate their children, and according to the medical community, consequently increase the population's risk of disease. Arguments against vaccines include the idea that large pharmaceutical companies that manufacture the vaccines are corrupt and lobby for vaccine laws just to make money. There has also been increased interest in natural health and the idea that you can be healthy without medicines. But the biggest complaint is that vaccines are administered by force.

Logan Molyneux, "Parents, Officials Struggle over Right to Refuse Vaccines," *Provo (UT) Daily Herald*, November 11, 2007. Reproduced by permission.

Laws in every state require school-aged children to receive a series of vaccine shots. Because there is overwhelming medical evidence and opinion stating that vaccines are not only safe but the greatest triumph of public health in history, many who choose not to vaccinate do so quietly and don't speak out about it for fear of being seen as a bad parent.

At 7 years old, Dylan is still non-verbal despite early intervention programs and thousands of dollars in therapy. Hansen said she never noticed any previous reaction to Dylan's or her other children's vaccinations. Dylan probably would have experienced various delays no matter what, she said, but she can't shake the idea that something changed that day. The experience scared her so bad she says none of her children will receive another vaccine, if she can help it. . . .

## Growing Numbers Seeking Exemptions

Immunization programs are becoming victims of their own success, [director of Utah County Health Department Dr. Joseph] Miner said, because as contagious diseases disappear, parents see less of a need to vaccinate their children. A recent Associated Press study found a rise in religious exemptions in states that don't allow philosophical exemptions. Some parents admitted their real concerns were about the safety of the vaccines, not their religious beliefs.

---

*Most of the resistance [to vaccination] revolves around the freedom of making an informed choice.*

---

The increasing exemptions are a problem for everyone, because vaccines are only effective to the extent that everyone gets them. Dr. Russell J. Osguthorpe, a pediatric infectious disease specialist at Utah Valley Regional Medical Center in Provo, likens it to requiring everyone to drive the speed limit so everyone has a safe ride.

"We don't immunize just for fun, or because we can," Osguthorpe said. "It's because children die from preventable diseases."

A 2000 study of Colorado children found that those who filed religious or philosophical exemptions were 22 times more likely to acquire measles and six times more likely to acquire pertussis (whooping cough) than vaccinated children. [In 2005], Utah Valley saw an outbreak of whooping cough—the county health department recorded more than seven times the normal amount of cases. Those sick kids can spread disease even to vaccinated children.

"Vaccines are between 95 and 99 percent effective," Miner said. "You've got anywhere from 1 to 5 percent of kids who for some reason have lost immunity or haven't developed it. That's a small percentage, but if you have 25 percent of other kids not immunized, then illness can spread through the whole population."

That's why Miner says deciding not to immunize your children puts them and their peers at risk. With 95 percent of the population in Utah Valley immune, there is little risk of an epidemic. But if that percentage continues growing, the risk would increase, and Miner said the state would have to disallow exemptions to protect the population.

## The Issue Is Freedom of Choice

Robert Johnston, an associate professor of history at the University of Illinois–Chicago, has studied the anti-vaccination movement for 20 years and said most of the resistance revolves around the freedom of making an informed choice.

"This is really the only area of American medical life that they're not allowed to offer a truly free consent," Johnston said. "Some of them may even vaccinate, but they may speak out for the right to choose. They're willing to hear that vaccines are safe, but they want to make that freedom of choice."

Interestingly, mandatory vaccination is one of the rare laws in society that citizens can choose not to follow. No one can declare themselves exempt from the speed limit, for example. So it's a push for freedom of choice in an area of public policy where adherence is already optional.

Why make a law and then allow people to break it? First, because here in the U.S., people value personal freedoms and rights so highly. Also, Brigham Young University public policy specialist Sven Wilson said the law sets an expectation of society, and even if it is optional, it encourages people to follow a particular path. Even an optional law has a greater influence than guidelines.

But vaccine skeptics say parents should do their homework before taking their children down the shot path.

"When you make a decision that involves a risk, you want to be the best parent and have the best information possible," said Barbara Loe Fisher, president of the National Vaccine Information Center, a leading vaccine skeptic group. "Vaccines should not be separated from the informed consent ethic in medicine. We recommend that parents do their homework and talk to one or more health professionals and get all the information they can." ...

It's precisely the overwhelming medical and public support for vaccines that vaccine skeptic Fisher says drives some parents to hide their choice.

"You have people telling you you're unpatriotic and selfish when you're just trying to protect your child," Fisher said. "Parents who do not vaccinate their children are seen as selfish, and they're talked about as a danger to public health. And when they use a religious exemption to get out of it, they're called liars. So the problem is that when parents talk about this they can then be targeted by their communities."

Driving those who choose not to vaccinate underground is not the goal of public health officials like Utah County's Dr. Miner. He said his work is a constant effort to educate.

"You have to constantly educate people about what it used to be like with infant mortality and preventable diseases," Miner said. "But unfortunately it takes an outbreak of whooping cough to remind people that this is what our grandparents were talking about when you used to have six or 10 kids in order to raise four of them to adulthood. Now we take it for granted that we'll raise all of them to adulthood, but that's not the way it used to be."

Osguthorpe said his work has introduced him to many cases of children afflicted with one of the 27 vaccine-preventable diseases. He speaks of them as tragedies, but tragedies that could have been averted with a timely vaccination.

"I'm confused by people who don't vaccinate their kids," Osguthorpe said. "They're playing dice with their kid, if you look at the chances. As I see cases of preventable diseases, and I talk with the moms and dads, when I tell them that it was preventable, they're just so sad and wish it could be so different. I'd like to see people avoid some of the heartache that is avoidable." . . .

## A History of Resistance

This is not the first time in Utah's history that there has been resistance to vaccines. An outbreak of smallpox in the late 1890s triggered a statewide vaccine controversy that lasted many years.

At the time, it had been more than 100 years since Edward Jenner first discovered a smallpox vaccine, but vaccination was not required in Utah. More than three years before the turn of the century, Utah saw 3,000 cases of smallpox and 26 deaths from the disease. Neighboring states, which by then had much success with the smallpox vaccine, complained that Utah was spreading the disease to the rest of the Intermountain West.

The state health commissioner, Theodore B. Beatty, enacted a mandatory vaccination ordinance. Even in the face of an epidemic, there was immediate, statewide opposition to the measure. The state Legislature passed a bill to repeal the mandatory vaccination requirement, and the governor quickly vetoed it. The Legislature just as swiftly overturned his veto and vaccination wasn't required in Utah until many years later.

Some of the backlash can be explained by a prevailing sentiment that The Church of Jesus Christ of Latter-day Saints was opposed to vaccinations. This was not the case, as is demonstrated by a May 1900 statement from church president Lorenzo Snow urging members to get vaccinated.

But an editor at the church-owned *Deseret News* frequently spoke out against vaccines, saying they were worse than the disease itself. Despite the president's statement, anti-vaccine sentiment held a firm position in Utah for decades.

By the 1930s, smallpox cases in Utah had significantly decreased, but there were still more cases than elsewhere. States that had mandatory vaccination laws in place weren't seeing any cases at all. Now the disease has been all but eradicated. The same goes for polio—there have been no cases of the crippling ailment in the United States since 1979.

"The success of these vaccines is huge," Osguthorpe said. "They're one of the greatest success stories of our time."

# Meningitis Vaccination Should Be Mandatory for College Dorm Residents

*Katie Strickland*

*Katie Strickland is a staff writer for the* Daily Bruin, *the newspaper of the University of California at Los Angeles.*

Did you know that there is a disease that could kill you within hours of contracting it—and could leave you brain damaged or an amputee if you managed to survive?

Allow me to introduce you to bacterial meningitis, an infection that landed two Texas A&M University students in the hospital in "very serious condition" [in October 2007]. This situation would have likely been prevented if Texas A&M made meningitis vaccinations mandatory for its incoming classes—a policy the University of California should enact immediately.

## Meningitis Can Be Deadly

According to the Centers for Disease Control and Prevention—the CDC—meningitis is an infection of the fluid surrounding the spinal cord and brain.

Although not as contagious as the flu, bacterial meningitis can still be spread through coughing, kissing or sharing drinking cups or cigarettes.

Because of this, freshmen who live in dormitories are classified by the CDC as being at a particularly "high risk" for contracting meningitis.

As someone who has lived in the cubicles that UCLA tries to pass off as dorm rooms, I know firsthand how limited personal space is in the residence halls. I was never more than a foot away from my two roommates and we often shared beverages and food—not to mention the floor-wide bathrooms and showers.

Katie Strickland, "UC Should Take Shot at Mandating Vaccine," *Daily Bruin*, October 11, 2007. Reproduced by permission.

It's easy to see how your average college dorm resident would be much more likely than the average person to pick up any sort of contagion.

Unlike an annoying floor-wide cold, however, meningitis is deadly, though completely treatable if caught early. What makes meningitis so terrifying is that nearly all of its symptoms mimic that of a common flu. By the time the distressed patient's symptoms become so worrisome [that] he or she seeks medical attention, the infection may have already become deadly.

The vaccine, properly known as the meningococcal vaccine, guards against two of the three types of meningitis in the US, and protects 90 percent of those who receive it, according to the CDC, which recommends that all people between the ages of 11 and 18, as well as college dorm dwellers, get vaccinated.

Yet most students I've spoken with don't even know what meningitis is and, therefore, never get vaccinated because they're not required to.

It is for this reason that the University of California should make the vaccine mandatory for all incoming students. Simply spreading awareness will not be sufficient motivation for students to seek out the vaccine on their own.

When proposing a mandatory vaccine, people generally bristle at the thought of being told what to do with their bodies.

## Putting the Whole Community at Risk

Yet choosing not to get a meningitis vaccine not only puts you at risk, but your whole community, since meningitis is contagious—even to some of those who have already been vaccinated. Rachel Futterman, a University of South Florida sophomore who received the vaccine her freshman year, died of meningitis.

Additionally, the risk associated with the vaccine is no greater than your average required inoculation and can even be given to pregnant women. The CDC reports the risk of "serious" side effects, such as harm or death, as "extremely small."

---

*Sometimes, in order to receive the benefits of living in a community, you must in turn make compromises for the health and safety of the group.*

---

The risk seems a great deal more insignificant when you consider that one in every four adolescents infected with meningitis will die, and 20 percent of survivors will be left with permanent disabilities, according to ABC News. The report also added that a "majority" of meningitis cases are "vaccine-preventable."

Before you begin panicking, however, keep in mind that bacterial meningitis is relatively uncommon, striking up to 3,000 Americans every year, according to ABC.

It seems a shame, however, for even one person's life to end or be forever limited by brain damage due to a generally preventable infection.

That is why this vaccine must be made mandatory. Exceptions can be made for those the CDC deigns unfit to receive the vaccine. For instance, the severely ill, or those with an allergy could be exempted from the mandated vaccination. But the rest of the incoming students should be made to provide proof of inoculation. If you still don't want the vaccine, that's fine, you don't have to live in the dorms.

Sometimes, in order to receive the benefits of living in a community, you must in turn make compromises for the health and safety of the group.

A little shot doesn't seem like too much to ask.

# All Young Girls Should Be Vaccinated to Prevent Cervical Cancer

*Elizabeth M. Whelan*

*Elizabeth M. Whelan is president of the American Council on Science and Health, an independent nonprofit consumer education consortium.*

The Food and Drug Administration approved the first vaccine specifically designed to prevent cancer [in June 2006]. Merck's Gardasil thwarts cervical cancer by blocking infection by the human papilloma virus, which is spread through sexual contact. Gardasil also blocks precancerous lesions that can cause infertility.

To reach maximum effectiveness, the drug should be administered at a young age—ideally between 9 and 14—to assure protection prior to sexual activity and to take advantage of the robust immune response among preteen girls.

Given that a half-million women in the U.S. are diagnosed with cervical cancer annually—and some 4,000 die from it—the approval of this drug is phenomenally good news. It is even better news for the developing world where cervical cancer is far more common than it is here. So it's all systems go, let's get all young girls vaccinated so we can wipe out cervical cancer in the U.S., right? Not quite.

The potential obstacle for widespread application of this new, life-saving vaccine is a concern that giving it to preteen girls will somehow be interpreted as a green light for early sexual activity.

Some religious-right groups, including Focus on the Family and the Family Research Council, while not opposed to the approval of Gardasil, adamantly oppose including Gardasil on the list of mandated inoculations required for public school attendance (such as diphtheria, mumps, and pertussis).

Opponents argue the disease is not communicable like mumps and measles and should be fought through "proper behavior" (meaning postponing all sexual encounters until marriage to a similarly inexperienced and uninfected man and remaining monogamous thereafter). As a spokesman for Focus on the Family put it, "We support the widespread availability of the vaccine, but we do oppose the mandatory vaccines for entry into public schools. . . . This is a disease that is completely sexually transmitted. . . . We believe that parents should have the final say on whether to vaccinate their children."

## Vaccination Is Medical, Not Moral Matter

Even the most libertarian must agree [that] certain public health mandates—such as laws requiring water chlorination and regulations demanding preschool vaccinations—have virtually wiped out life-threatening communicable and infectious diseases. These interventions represent "public health" at its best. If we gave everyone the choice of whether to vaccinate their kids, we would have disease profiles approaching those of the Third World.

The argument that cervical cancer is "different" because it is largely sexually transmitted and therefore it can be prevented through strict sexual abstinence is just plain naive. Even the relatively small percentage of women who do remain sexually inactive until marriage will run the risk of exposure from their husbands.

The use of Gardasil is a medical matter—not a moral one.

The mere fact that 10- or 14-year-old girls are inoculated with Gardasil has nothing to do with their propensity to commence sexual activity. Those decisions are culturally and religiously based—and can be very much influenced by parents—

with or without Gardasil. Clearly there are myriad reasons for young, immature youth of either sex to postpone sexual relationships. These include the risk of numerous sexually transmitted diseases (from which Gardasil offers no protection), negative emotional effects, and distraction from high priorities like education, not to mention the very real risk of unwanted pregnancy. What parent could possibly argue that a vaccination at age 10 would increase the odds of promiscuity when there are so many other real-life reasons not to become sexually active at a young age?

> *Protection from cervical cancer and youthful sexual abstinence can happily coexist.*

We should be able to alleviate ethical concerns by taking three complementary steps:

1. Make it well known that the new vaccine, when used appropriately, will virtually eliminate cervical cancer.

2. Stress that the reason it must be given early in life is that inoculation at that point provides the best chance of lifetime protection (we do not know if booster shots will be necessary later in life).

3. Completely separate the medical matter—preventing cancer—from moral matters regarding premarital sex.

Perhaps Merck can circumvent this controversy: while promoting the inclusion of Gardasil as a standard or required form of vaccination, the company might also work with family-focused groups who oppose sex outside marriage to co-develop educational tools for discouraging premature sexual relationships—citing medical, emotional, and practical reasons for doing so.

Protection from cervical cancer and youthful sexual abstinence can happily coexist.

# Making Cervical Cancer Vaccination Mandatory Is Bad Medicine

*Lucinda Marshall*

*Lucinda Marshall is a feminist artist, writer, and activist. She is the founder of the Feminist Peace Network.*

Governor Rick Perry's decision to sidestep the Texas legislature and issue an executive order mandating that girls entering the 6th grade receive the new HPV [human papillomavirus] vaccine raises troubling questions about the influence pharmaceutical companies wield on the crafting of public health policy. Cervical cancer is only expected to cause 3670 deaths in the US in 2007, a miniscule percentage (less than 2%) of the 270,000 deaths from the disease worldwide and only 1% of the total annual number of deaths from all cancers in the United States.

While cervical cancer used to be one of the deadliest diseases for women in the US, the number of deaths it causes has dropped dramatically (by 74% from 1955-1992) and it continues to drop. Why then are so many states considering mandating a vaccine that costs $300–$500 per patient for a type of cancer that is already largely under control in this country and which can be almost entirely prevented by regular gynecological checkups and Pap smears?

## Financial Motives

Merck & Co., the giant pharmaceutical company that makes the vaccine Gardasil, is spending millions of dollars lobbying state legislators. In Texas, where Merck recently doubled its

Lucinda Marshall, "Making the HPV Vaccine Mandatory Is Bad Medicine," *Dissident Voice* (www.dissidentvoice.org), February 8, 2007. Reproduced by permission of the author.

lobbying efforts, Gov. Perry received $6000 from Merck's political action committee during his last campaign. One of Merck's key lobbyists in Texas is Perry's former chief-of-staff and the mother-in-law of his current chief-of-staff is the state director of Women in Government, a national advocacy group of female state legislators that has received substantial funds from Merck.

It is important to note that low income women and women who do not have health insurance are most at risk because they are less likely to get regular Pap smears. More than half of the diagnosed cases of cervical cancer are in women who have not had a Pap smear in three years. While Gov. Perry has mandated that the state of Texas foot the bill for those who can't afford the expensive HPV vaccine, it is unclear where those funds would come from either in Texas or in other states that are considering making the vaccine mandatory. And obviously the cost of the vaccine makes it prohibitive in the countries where it is most needed and would potentially do the most good.

What is clear is that Merck has a substantial financial interest in the vaccine becoming mandatory even though the added benefit to public health is both minimal and costly. With more than 10 million girls in the US between the ages of 10 and 14, the drug company stands to make billions of dollars preventing a disease that is already treatable in the targeted population. Since the vaccine does not eliminate the need for regular Pap smears, it would appear that a far more appropriate and cost effective first step would be to make regular gynecological healthcare available for all women regardless of income and medical insurance, particulary since this step by itself would go a long way in reducing the few cases of cervical cancer that still occur in this country.

## Potential Risks of the Vaccine

There is however another significant public health concern in regard to the HPV vaccine, namely that it is a very new drug with no history. We are of course being told that it is perfectly safe and has few side effects, but we were also told that about Thalidomide, DES [diethylstilbestrol, a synthetic estrogen] and Hormone Replacement Therapy [all of which were found to have bad side effects]. Negative health concerns have also been raised about other children's vaccines and the anthrax vaccine given to those in the armed forces as well as drugs like Vioxx [a nonsteroidal anti-inflamatory drug, which was recalled], another Merck drug.

*It seems unconscionable to mandate the use of a vaccine that has the potential to put the lives and health of an entire generation of girls at risk.*

While Merck says that Gardasil is 100% effective in preventing the two types of the HPV that cause 70% of all cervical cancer, questions have arisen about these results. In an article in *Healthfacts*, Maryann Napoli, associate director of the Center for Medical Consumers reports that according to Barbara Loe Fisher, president of the National Vaccine Information Center and a former member of the FDA [Food and Drug Administration] Vaccines and Related Biologic Products Advisory Committee, the placebos in Merck's studies contained aluminum (which is reported to cause inflammation and cell death in animals and humans) rather than saline solution, which according to Fisher "violates the principle of scientific method . . . making it hard to tell whether the many adverse events reported were due to the use of aluminum in both the placebo and the drug or to the Gardasil itself."

And in an essay published in the *New York Times* in July 2006, Rent Rabin points out that most of the subjects in the Merck trials were women over the age of 16. Rabin found that the vaccine was only tested on 1,200 girls under the age of 16. In addition, the vaccine is so new that it is not yet known for how long it will be effective or whether a booster will be required. It is also important to note that Merck's own literature states that Gardasil, "has not been evaluated for the potential to cause carcinogenicity or genotoxicity."

It is not that guarding against HPV is not a good idea, in theory of course it is a great idea, but a healthy dose of skepticism is appropriate when it comes to believing the promises or stated motives of pharmaceutical companies. It seems unconscionable to mandate the use of a vaccine that has the potential to put the lives and health of an entire generation of girls at risk for the sake of preventing a cancer that is a risk to so few young women in this country and which, can already be prevented by other less risky means.

# The Chickenpox Vaccine Is Unnecessary and Its Safety Is Unproven

*Andrew Schlafly*

*Andrew Schlafly, a nationally known attorney, is general counsel to the American Association of Physicians and Surgeons. He is also a noted teacher of online homeschooling classes.*

The Association of American Physicians & Surgeons, Inc. ("AAPS"), founded in 1943, is a nationwide group of thousands of physicians. We oppose the proposed mandate for vaccination against chickenpox.

Prior to the development of the varicella (chickenpox) vaccine, the disease was widely recognized to be one of the most benign illnesses. For example, *Encyclopedia of Medicine* of the American Medical Association stated in 1989 that chickenpox is a "common and mild infectious disease of childhood" and that "all healthy children should be exposed to chickenpox ... at an age at which it is no more than an inconvenience." Likewise, the American Academy of Pediatrics declared in a 1996 brochure that "[m]ost children who are otherwise healthy and get chickenpox won't have any complications from the disease."

## Risk from Chickenpox Is Low

Indeed, the chickenpox fatality rate is among the lowest of all known diseases, with only about 100 dying out of millions who contract chickenpox each year. Moreover, most of those fatalities are in adults rather than children. For example, a study published in the *British Medical Journal* on July 27,

Andrew Schafly, "Testimony to New Jersey Department of Health," aapsonline.org, May 12, 2003. Reproduced by permission of Association of American Physicians and Surgeons, Inc.

2002, confirmed that 81% of the deaths attributable to chickenpox over a recent 12-year period in Britain were adults, not children.

The risk of contracting and dying from chickenpox is little more than the risk of being struck and killed by lightning, which is about 89 per year in the U.S. Nevertheless, those adults who are concerned about such a low health risk may obtain the varicella vaccine voluntarily. The vaccine manufacturer can advertise, and consumers can make their own decisions. Over time, the free market would force improvements in the cost and efficacy of the vaccine, and the consumer will be better off for it.

But what we object to here is the forcing of children to take this vaccine at public expense. Children have nothing to fear from the disease, and should not be forced by law to undergo unnecessary medical treatment. The varicella vaccine is still relatively new and unproven, both in safety and efficacy. Forcing millions to receive this vaccine, at substantial expense, would constitute an experiment on the public. Given the scarcity of money for medical care, our dollars are much better spent where people actually want the services.

The FDA Summary for Basis of Approval (SBA) . . . conceals key data comparing the vaccine to the placebo. Nevertheless, the limited posted data about vaccine side effects are themselves alarming. For example, the data disclose that post-vaccine fatigue was reported in 27.4% of recipients in healthy children and 29% of healthy adolescents and adults; post-vaccine chills were reported in 4.8% of children and 8.7% of adolescents and adults; abdominal pain was reported in 8.2% of children and 7.7% of adolescents and adults; disturbed sleep in 24.1% of children and 15.6% of adolescents and adults; eye complaints in 6.2% of children and 8.5% of adults; and so on. These side effects are alone worthy of concern, and also suggest the likelihood of more serious injury.

This report ignores side effects occurring beyond 42 days of receipt of the vaccine, such as exacerbated asthma, diabetes or autism. Shingles is also a serious problem connected with the vaccine.

Against these significant adverse effects, what are a child's chances of being injured by the disease? Less than 1 in one million die from chickenpox annually, and it is unlikely most children today will ever contract the disease. A study of 3000 children in 11 daycare centers between 1995 and 1997 was published in "Conference Coverage (ICAAC) Unvaccinated Children Protected, But May Pay Later," *Immunotherapy Weekly*, Oct 12, 1998. Despite being in group care, chickenpox among the children studied was zero among children age 1 to 2 years, 5 percent in children age 2 to 3 years, and 13 percent in children age 3 to 4 years.

---

*Vaccine manufacturers force their goods on kids, who do not need them, while failing to persuade adults to buy them in a free market.*

---

In a survey of pediatricians published in August 1998 in the *Archives of Pediatrics & Adolescent Medicine*, it was found that only 42% adhered to a report by the American Academy of Pediatrics recommending universal varicella vaccination of children. Why would New Jersey require a universal treatment that most pediatricians feel is unjustified?

## Companies Profit from Mandated Products

The reason is profit for the companies selling the mandated products. Children need vaccines only 1/100th as much as adults, yet childhood vaccinations account for 65% of the multibillion dollar annual U.S. vaccine market. Vaccine manufacturers force their goods on kids, who do not need them, while failing to persuade adults to buy them in a free market. As with other vaccine mandates, disease data based on adults are used to force vaccines on children. There is no evidence that the vaccines will even remain effective into adulthood for those children. In the SBA for the varicella vaccine (cited above), Merck admits that "[t]he duration of protection of VARIVAX is unknown at present and the need for booster doses is not defined."

In addition, New Jersey does not have a philosophical exemption to these vaccine mandates and the varicella vaccine is a highly objectionable one on moral grounds. The vaccine was developed based on having been "serially passaged through primary human embryonic lung culture" (quoting the SBA cited above). The published SBA, however, has deleted and drawn a huge "X" through its explanation of the details of how human embryos were used in developing this vaccine. All indications are that the varicella vaccine was developed through use of abortion. Parents in New Jersey have a right to know the details, and there should not be mandatory vaccination of a morally offensive vaccine. A majority of New Jerseyans adhere to religions that reject abortion; why should they be forced to receive a vaccine based on it?

It is worth noting that the *Physicians Desk Reference* contains this warning: "Vaccine recipients should attempt to avoid, whenever possible, close association with susceptible high-risk individuals for up to six weeks. . . . Susceptible high-risk individuals include immunocompromised individuals; pregnant women without documented history of chickenpox or laboratory evidence of prior infection; newborn infants of mothers without documented history of chickenpox or laboratory evidence of prior infection." Thus this Department is proposing a mandate that creates a serious risk of harm, without legal remedy for the injured victims. AAPS strongly opposes this proposal.

Three months into the federally mandated smallpox inoculation, the federal government has recently permitted states to terminate the program if they choose. Only 35,000 of the half-million targeted workers had received the smallpox vaccine before it became necessary to reverse the mandate. In that relatively short period of time the smallpox mandate caused eleven cases of unusual heart inflammation, three civilian deaths, plus the unexplained death of NBC correspondent David Bloom within weeks of receiving the smallpox vaccine. Earlier, the federal government also had to reverse its mandate for the rotavirus vaccine after infants tragically and unnecessarily died from it. New Jerseyans should not be forced down the same road with a mandatory chickenpox vaccine.

# New Jersey's New Childhood Vaccine Mandates Are Indefensible

*Deirdre Imus*

*Deirdre Imus is the founder and president of the Deirdre Imus Environmental Center for Pediatric Oncology. She writes a blog at www.huffingtonpost.com, the Web site of the* Huffington Post *online newspaper.*

Albert Einstein once said, "only two things are infinite: the universe and human stupidity." We got a good dose of what many would call "human stupidity" . . . in New Jersey when 5 un-elected members of the Public Health Council (PHC) voted to mandate four new vaccines for children. The vaccines that will be mandated in 2008 include: the influenza vaccine, pneumococcal, meningococcal, tetanus, diphtheria and acellular pertussis (Tdap) vaccine. Two of the vaccines, influenza and Sanofi Pasteur's meningococcal vaccine (Menomune) contain thimerosal (mercury).

In spite of a week's-long protest from constituents that included parents, physicians and dozens of organizations, the State Health Commissioner gave his "seal of approval" on Friday, December 15 [2007].

Today I want to appeal to New Jersey Governor [J.] Corzine to re-evaluate these recommendations and carefully consider the ramifications for New Jersey's children.

Unless Governor Corzine, the state legislature, or perhaps a judge intervenes, New Jersey will go down in history as the first state in the nation, for that matter the world, to order parents to vaccinate their preschoolers with a known develop-

Deirdre Imus, "Missing the Mercury Threat: An Appeal to New Jersey's Governor," *Huffington Post*, December 21, 2007. Reproduced by permission.

mental neurotoxin, which many parents, physicians and scientific research suggest is linked to the epidemic of developmental disorders, including autism.

## Mercury Is Toxic

The PHC recommendation came just days before another "first in the nation" law was passed by Minnesota lawmakers who voted to ban the use of mercury in mascara and other cosmetics. "Mercury does cause neurological damage to people even in tiny quantities . . . [and] can retard brain development in children and fetuses who are most vulnerable to the metal's toxic effects," stated the Minnesota officials.

That's right, you can't put mercury on your mommy's lashes in Minnesota but New Jersey health officials just can't wait to inject it into your young children.

After repeated warnings about mercury toxicity in fish and following its removal from over the counter products, thermostats, industrial switches, medical devices, animal vaccines, even a leg paint used on horses, the five appointed members of the PHC and the NJ Department of Health (DOH) can claim credit for what could be one of the worst and ill-advised public health decisions forced upon the public in recent memory; a decision that was made under a cloak of secrecy, without sufficient debate and perhaps in violation of procedural protocols.

New Jersey parents have a right to question the DOH actions. After all New Jersey holds the dubious honor of having the highest autism rates in the country. According to the Centers for Disease Control and Prevention (CDC), one in 94 New Jersey children have autism, 1 in 60 boys.

While some NJ public health officials arrogantly dismiss the link between vaccines and autism as "scientifically unfounded," and tell reporters concerns about thimerosal is "a moot issue," since most vaccines are either free of the compound or contain only trace amounts, like the preschool flu vaccine, a growing body of published scientific research shows this opinion cannot be factually supported.

To the contrary, approximately 90% of the influenza vaccine supply still contains thimerosal. According to the FDA [Food and Drug Administration], the 25 micrograms of mercury in one influenza vaccine is *not* a "trace amount." According to EPA [Environmental Protection Agency] guidelines, this amount can only be considered safe if a person weighs 550 pounds. You would think a health official would know this.

## Not Effective for Young Children

In addition, there is no convincing evidence that the flu shot is actually effective. A study published in the *British Medical Journal*, done by the Cochran Collaboration, considered the Gold Standard for scientific research, stated the recommendations of flu shots for infants and toddlers are not backed by scientific evidence [Jan.25, 2006]. So if research tells us the vaccine is ineffective and it contains toxic mercury, why are officials recommending it be given to our young children?

Sanofi's Menactra meningococcal vaccine is thimerosal-free and currently recommended for children between 11 and 12 years old. However, the FDA and the CDC are investigating cases of Guillain-Barré syndrome (GBS) among adolescents who received this vaccine. A larger study led by Harvard Pilgrim Healthcare is expected to take approximately 2 years. According to the CDC, "The study period is necessary to accumulate cases and attain sufficient statistical power."

The recommended acceptable alternative is Sanofi's Menomune, which contains 25 micrograms of thimerosal, thus adding to the overall body burden of one of the most toxic metals on earth.

While some officials want to continue dismissing the vaccine-autism association, the neurological risks associated with the use of the mercury-based preservative have been well documented in the scientific literature for decades.

This is noted in a 2004 California Environmental Protection Agency Office of Environmental Health Hazard Assessment that found: "the scientific evidence that [thimerosal] cause[s] reproductive toxicity is clear and voluminous.... The evidence for its reproductive toxicity includes severe mental retardation or malformations in human offspring who were poisoned when their mothers were exposed to ethyl mercury or thimerosal while pregnant." ...

The National Toxicology Program (NTP) states that thimerosal is "poison by ingestion, subcutaneous, intravenous and possibly other routes," and warns that childhood exposure could result in "mental retardation in children, loss of coordination in speech, writing, gait, stupor, and irritability and bad temper progressing to mania."

A 1984 study published in the *Journal of Pediatrics* found, "Thimerosal used to irrigate the external auditory canals in a child with tympanostomy tubes [a small tube inserted into the eardrum] has caused severe mercury poisoning."

In 2001 the American Academy of Pediatrics (AAP) published a review on the state of science related to mercury toxicity entitled, "Technical Report: Mercury in the Environment: Implications for Pediatricians." The report concluded, "Mercury in all of its forms is toxic to the fetus and children.... Inorganic and elemental mercury should not be present in the home or other environments of children.... It would seem prudent for the FDA to carefully examine all uses of mercury in pharmaceuticals, particularly pharmaceuticals that are used by infants and pregnant women."

As recently as [November 2007] a study published in the *Journal of Child Neurology* determined, "a significant relation does exist between the blood levels of mercury and diagnosis of an autism spectrum disorder."

## Not All Physicians Favor Flu Shots

New Jersey's health officials may believe giving preschoolers and other children mercury-containing influenza shots is good public health policy but not all physicians would agree. Many physicians, including United States Congressman Dave Weldon (R-FL), a strong supporter of our nation's immunization program, has gone on record stating, "Any doctor who would knowingly inject a baby with a mercury-containing vaccine, I would consider that malpractice."

If these are not reason enough to question the new mandates, just last month [November 2007] one of the first autism cases presented in the U.S. Court of Federal Claims (vaccine court), the government *conceded* that vaccines aggravated a pre-existing mitochondrial dysfunction causing autistic like symptoms in one of the first cases where the case filed was a claim that thimerosal caused autism.

So please don't tell me the link between vaccines and autism is "scientifically unfounded," or there is "no evidence" that vaccines cause autism in some children. The federal government has already conceded this point in one case.

Mercury is not the only problem with the new mandates.

The Prevnar pneumococcal vaccine also has its own problems. There have been 3,243 adverse reactions reported to the government's vaccine surveillance system since Prevnar was first licensed in 2000. These reports included 476 serious reactions and 79 deaths. Just a few months ago the Prevnar vaccine was linked to a new antibiotic resistant "superbug" bacterial infection, causing serious ear infections in children as young as 6 months. One child suffered permanent hearing loss.

Should health officials be forcing parents to give their children vaccines that contain a heavy metal toxin whose packaging contains the universal symbol for poison and warns the product could cause mental retardation or one that has thousands of reported adverse reactions? Where do we draw the line on who knows what is best for our own children?

In response to the Public Health Council's recommendations, Governor Corzine was quoted that he does not "in any way think we should take risks on vaccines . . . the elements of evaluation should be left to scientists and data."

I couldn't agree more with Governor Corzine on this point. Ultimately it is the Governor who is responsible and I am hopeful that he is taking this matter very seriously.

---

*Vaccines have become the lifeblood of the pharmaceutical industry.*

---

No governor wants to reject the recommendations of their public health officials. However, Governor Corzine would not be the first one to do so in this situation.

When faced with the recommendation by California health officials to veto a bill aimed at banning thimerosal from children's vaccines back in 2004, Governor Arnold Schwarzenegger rejected this advice and signed the Mercury Free Act, which strictly limits the amount of mercury in vaccines or products used by pregnant women and very young children in the state of California. In a signing message, Schwarzenegger stated, "I believe that an abundance of caution merits the acceleration of the process already underway to remove thimerosal from the last few vaccines that contain it."

Six other governors have signed into law similar bills overruling the objections of public health officials.

## All About Money

Look, everyone knows what these new recommendations are all about. *Money, money, and more money!*

Vaccines have become the lifeblood of the pharmaceutical industry.

In the 2004 annual report for Chiron Corporation, sales of their flu vaccine went from $90 million in 2002 to $332.4 million in 2003. Total vaccine sales went from $357.4 million (2002) to $678.3 million (2003). Nice increase.

I note this particular year's report because it was in 2003 that industry, along with health officials, aggressively forged ahead with a masterful marketing plan. Create fear that terrible diseases are going to spread through schools like wildfires if every kid isn't vaccinated through a very well financed lobbying and advertising campaign. Then get a handful of health officials to "rubber stamp" exactly what the industry wants. What corporation wouldn't covet a program sanctioned by the government that forces the public to use their products?

The profits from mandated vaccines has resulted in billions of [dollars] for the drug companies and if enacted, the new vaccine recommendations will deliver billions more.

An easy and guaranteed flow of revenue for industry and physicians alike.

It wouldn't surprise me at all to learn that certain members of the Public Health Council were the recipients of pharmaceutical industry generosity. (Riki Jacobs [a member of the New Jersey Health Council] received [pharmaceutical giant] Pfizer money for her AIDS foundation).

---

*The state has not needed to mandate these vaccines in the past and there is no public health emergency to warrant the implementation of the recommendations now.*

---

For the record, I have repeatedly acknowledged the importance of vaccinations. There is no question that vaccines have saved many lives but they are not without risks. Over the last decade, however, serious and legitimate questions have arisen regarding the number of vaccines we are giving our children today and whether the ingredients in those vaccines are as safe as we, the public, have been led to believe. Until these safety concerns are addressed in a transparent manner, parents, not bureaucrats, should decide what is best for their children.

In January of [2007], in response to mercury contamination at a children's day care center, Governor Corzine signed a bill that would enforce strict guidelines to ensure environmental safety at child care centers and schools. In a statement Governor Corzine said, "This puts New Jersey at the forefront of states nationally in protecting children from environmental contaminants while at child care facilities and schools."

It would be the height of hypocrisy for New Jersey to now tell parents they must inject their children with mercury-containing vaccines.

It is time for New Jersey to lead the nation again and reject the new vaccine mandates and send a message that our children are no longer going to be the depositories for toxic contaminants in order to increase profits for the pharmaceutical industry.

Any parent who wants to vaccinate their child with any of the four new recommended vaccines can do so today without government coercion. The state has not needed to mandate these vaccines in the past and there is no public health emergency to warrant the implementation of the recommendations now. There is however a public health crisis in New Jersey caused by the rapid rise of developmental disorders, like autism.

There can be no harm in slowing down this process and carefully reviewing the mandated recommendations along with the current state of science, and the possible ramifications of this very aggressive vaccination policy.

The new vaccine mandates are not defensible in light of all we know about thimerosal and mercury toxicity. Governor Corzine has the legal authority and the responsibility to protect New Jersey's children from additional and unnecessary mercury exposure. [The mandate was passed by the New Jersey Public Health Council 5-2.]

# Compulsory Vaccination Eliminates Normal Checks on Government Power

## Mark Blaxill and Barbara Loe Fisher

*Mark Blaxill is the vice president of SafeMinds, a nonprofit organization founded to investigate and raise awareness of the risk from mercury in vaccines. Barbara Loe Fisher is the cofounder and president of the National Vaccine Information Center, a consumer-led vaccine safety advocacy organization.*

The rising complexity of vaccine risks and benefits makes the assessment of risk far more sensitive to the assessment of such complex trade-offs. But when the guardians of vaccine safety [at the CDC, the Centers for Disease Control and Prevention] play a dual role as advocates of program expansion, the potential for bias, conflict of interest and bureaucratic error in these assessments rise when there are no mechanisms in place for self-correction. When advocates of vaccine programs can also exercise the coercive power of the state to enforce their decisions through vaccine mandates, the risks of catastrophic failure multiply.

In an open society, we typically rely on the free choices of informed citizens as the corrective mechanism for dealing with complex trade-offs. We express our freedom in two ways, through the free market (for economic trade-offs) or free elections (for policy making). In either domain, we know from long experience that assigning decision rights to centralized state authorities can produce lasting inefficiencies and/or inappropriate concentrations of power. Checks and balances on such power are essential to prevent the abuse of power by the state and secure improved outcomes for society.

Mark Blaxill and Barbara Loe Fisher, "The Atlanta Manifesto, Part 5," *Age of Autism*, December 15, 2007. Reproduced by permission of the authors.

## Achieving Herd Immunity

Vaccine programs introduce special problems in an open society. Mass vaccination programs for infectious disease prevention are based on the premise that herd immunity is the only way to manage infectious diseases. Achieving herd immunity requires widespread compliance, indeed significantly greater compliance than either free markets or free elections require for success. Vaccination coverage rates sufficient to provide herd immunity have been estimated to be in the 80–95% range depending on the disease. Achieving such high compliance rates in large populations demands extraordinary efforts. Compounding this difficulty, public health officials have increasingly defined success as compliance rates approaching 100%, a shift from a goal of herd immunity to a goal of local elimination, even global eradication, of most diseases for which vaccines have been developed. With such aggressive targets the exercise of economic choice ("I don't want to receive that service") or the declaration of dissent ("I don't support that policy") runs in direct opposition to the interests of the bureaucracy in meeting its performance goals.

*Vaccine program sponsors ask for and typically receive exemptions from normal checks and balances on state power.*

In order to reach these rising compliance targets, vaccine program sponsors ask for and typically receive exemptions from normal checks and balances on state power. These exemptions are justified because the prevention of disease is seen as an area in which the interests of the collective override the rights of the individual. Consequently, manufacturers receive exemptions from product liability laws. Citizens face powerful sanctions if they fail to comply with state recommendations—children can be denied entry to school, parents can be declared negligent, and pediatricians can deny service to families when they choose not to vaccinate. Program managers are protected from accountability to external parties in numerous ways.

These exemptions can end up producing an unhealthy relationship between citizens and central authorities. In the eyes of the officials, a diverse and autonomous citizenry becomes a monolithic and (ideally) submissive "public." The public must be convinced of the virtues of compliance so that the herd can maintain its immunity and remain safe from disease. The more submissive the herd, the greater the opportunity for heroic achievements in disease elimination and the less the need to apply coercive measures to dissenting citizens.

## Extraordinary Exemptions

Yet the childhood immunization program is the only medical intervention capable of producing injury or death that the state imposes on healthy children. Vaccines are also the only privately manufactured product whose universal consumption is made a prerequisite for participation in public services. These extraordinary exemptions from our normal democratic system of checks and balances and free markets demand extraordinary, and constant, scrutiny. Vaccine program management must not only work when safety is secured, it must also be robust in the face of safety failures.

But how robust can our system of vaccine safety management ever be? If one assumes that program managers are always diligent, competent and correct in their assessments and that the programs themselves are unambiguously and universally safe, then these exemptions from our standards of openness are a small price to pay for results. But when there is a possibility of negligence, incompetence, or even well-intentioned error, these protections run the risk of perpetuating and exacerbating truly catastrophic failures. In their book, *The Virus and the Vaccine*, Deborah Bookchin and Jim Schumacher elaborated the dangers:

The decisions of our health policy makers, even when well intentioned are not always well informed. And sometimes those decisions are not even well intentioned. Sometimes they are based on bias or inadequate scientific evidence. Sometimes they are biased by the close relationship between the pharmaceutical industry and the government health officials who are charged with regulating that industry. Moreover, sometimes even the best scientists can make mistakes. The safest medical products can have unforeseen side effects. Things do occasionally go wrong, sometimes dreadfully wrong, during even the most noble of scientific endeavors.

And when things do go wrong, the inevitably defensive reactions can creep down a slippery slope from the prevention of unnecessary panic to the dissemination of propaganda and the suppression of dissent. The resources available to health officials to mount defenses in the face of failure are extensive. Prestigious journals can relax their standards in support of questionable research; at-risk constituencies can mobilize resources to attack discomforting facts; funding agencies can deny resources for investigations into possible failures; and conscientious scientists can face disincentives (even sanctions) when they pursue unpopular investigations.

## The Right of Informed Consent

One powerful bulwark against such breakdowns is the right of informed consent. Informed consent requires and empowers each citizen to make choices for themselves and their families based on their independent assessment of risks and benefits. Informed consent thereby provides a counterbalancing force against overreaching activities of the state and provides incentives for manufacturers to improve the safety and effectiveness of their products:

- In the absence of an ability to choose between vaccine formulations, combinations and producers, citizens can at least exercise choice with respect to timing and receipt of specific vaccinations;

- In the absence of meaningful product guarantees or warranties, citizens can request and expect the provision of scientific information regarding attributed risks and benefits of vaccines;

- In the absence of clear scientific knowledge regarding the immunological mechanisms, failure modes and adverse exposure consequences, citizens can seek, consider and act on information from multiple sources, reserving the right to critically review official interpretations of vaccine benefits and risks and freely act upon the information they have obtained.

Today, parents who wish to make a different choice with respect to their children's vaccinations face numerous obstacles. They can claim a medical exemption if their child has suffered a "severe vaccine reaction" that must meet restrictive CDC standards as a contraindication to further vaccination and are able to find a doctor willing to write a medical exemption to vaccination. They can, in most states, claim exemption based on sincerely held religious beliefs. In eighteen states, they can exercise their right to a philosophical or conscientious belief exemption to vaccination. But everywhere these rights might be exercised, they are, practically speaking, nearly impossible to obtain (in the case of medical exemptions), under challenge (religious exemptions) or available only to a small number of parents who are aware of their rights.

In real life, when parents resist their pediatrician's advice, they risk sanctions of varying severity, up to and including loss of medical care, health insurance and even custody. Pediatricians or nurses can and do notify Child Welfare authorities when parents resist vaccination and the parents can be charged with child medical neglect. Parents can postpone the age [of] vaccination, but in doing so they forego access to most child-care and educational services. Indeed, with respect to the universal hepatitis B birth dose, they often find that vaccination takes place in hospital nurseries without their knowledge, preceding consent. The provision of true informed consent, which has defined the ethical practice of modern medicine and is so essential as a counterweight to state power, remains a distant promise for most American parents.

# Push to Mandate New Vaccines Comes from Profit-Driven Industry

*Evelyn Pringle*

*Evelyn Pringle is an investigative reporter whose specialty is exposing corruption in government and corporate America.*

The push to keep adding more vaccines to the mandatory schedules comes directly from a purely profit motivated industry and a recent investor report estimates that the worldwide market will quadruple from about $4.3 billion in 2006 to more than $16 billion in 2016, with the biggest boost coming from kids in the US.

A November 2007 report entitled, "Pipeline and Commercial Insight: Pediatric and Adolescent Vaccines," authored by vaccine analyst, Hedwig Kresse, for the independent market analyst Datamonitor discusses the future outlook for vaccine profits.

The report provides an assessment of products and a patient-based forecast of market size and coverage rates to the year 2016, and predicts that the introduction of high-price vaccines will induce rapid growth in the pediatric and adolescent vaccines market.

The report predicts that due to the "promising commercial potential" of new, high-price vaccines, the pediatric and adolescent market will quadruple from approximately $4.3 billion in 2006, to over $16 billion by 2016, across the US; the EU [European Union]-five, including France, Germany, Italy, Spain, and the UK; and Japan.

Evelyn Pringle, "Time to End Profit-Driven Mandatory Vaccination Racket," *Scoop*, February 12, 2008. Reproduced by permission of the author.

## Mandatory Vaccines Mean
## Commercial Success

The crucial factor for success in the pediatric market, the report notes, is the introduction of a product into national vaccination schedules. "Along with reimbursement, this virtually guarantees the rapid uptake and continuously high coverage rates in the target population," Ms Kresse states.

As an example, she cites Wyeth's Prevnar, as the first premium price vaccine launched in the US in 2000 for vaccinating infants against pneumonia and meningitis.

Since then, Prevnar has been added to the childhood vaccination schedules in the US and EU-five despite its high price of nearly $320 for the 4-dose regimen. In 2006, global sales reached almost $2 billion, making Prevnar the first vaccine to attain blockbuster status, according to the report. By 2016, Datamonitor expects the total value of the infant market for pneumococcal vaccines to increase to $2.3 billion.

In June 2006, Merck's Gardasil was approved for [human papillomavirus, or HPV, which can cause] cervical cancer. Because it was the first vaccine offered as a preventive measure for a form of cancer, its approval generated tremendous public attention along with pressure for healthcare authorities to make the vaccine available to teenage girls at a cost of $360 for 3 doses.

"Although most cases of cervical cancer in the developed world can be prevented through the existing pap smear screening programs, the expensive HPV vaccination has been recommended and is reimbursed for teenage girls across the US and Europe," Ms Kresse reports.

She notes that this decision is driven more by public pressure and excitement about the opportunity to vaccinate against cancer rather than by real need. The widespread publicity has led to a good uptake in the target group of adolescent girls, which is usually hard to reach for vaccination, Ms Kresse points out to investors.

Datamonitor sees a huge commercial opportunity in HPV vaccines, with annual sales of $1.4 billion in teenage girls for the seven major markets by 2016 and a cumulative catch-up opportunity in women aged 13–26 that could add up to over $17 billion until 2016.

But Ms Kresse warns investors that the "lack of medical need" for rotavirus vaccines such as RotaTeq will limit their uptake in most markets. RotaTeq is advertised to combat diarrhea that usually affects infants under the age of two, and was introduced by Merck in the US in 2006, at a price of $200 for the three-dose regimen.

According to Ms Kresse, many countries, but not the US, have refused to add the vaccine to their schedules due to cost-benefit reasons. "In the developed world, rotavirus diarrhea is rarely severe for small infants and quick and efficacious treatment is already available," she writes. "Consequently, healthcare authorities see no need to widely introduce a very expensive vaccine."

Datamonitor estimates that annual sales will remain limited to approximately $1 billion across the 7 major markets by 2016 and predicts that the US will account for the majority of sales, being the only country to have recommended the rotavirus vaccine for all infants.

Wyeth's Prevnar vaccine came on the market in 2000 and is recommended for children under 2. The vaccine was hailed as a breakthrough and had sales of more than $1.5 billion in 2006. Prevnar is given as four shots to children between 2 and 15 months.

## Vaccines Promote Resistant Bacteria

On September 18, 2007, *NewsMax* reported that the vaccine has dramatically curbed pneumonia and other serious illnesses in children but is also having an unfortunate effect: "promoting new superbugs that cause ear infections."

According to *NewsMax*, doctors reported finding the first such germ that is resistant to all drugs approved to treat childhood ear infections and 9 toddlers in Rochester, N.Y., have had the bug and that it also may be turning up elsewhere.

---

*The established duration of immunity for vaccines is greatly underestimated, which means that people are getting booster shots when their immunity levels do not require it.*

---

It is a strain of strep bacteria not included in the pneumococcal vaccine. Prevnar prevents seven strains responsible for most cases of pneumonia, meningitis and bloodstream infections. But dozens more strains exist and some have become resistant to antibiotics since the vaccine combats the more common strains.

If the new strains continue to spread, "it tells us the vaccine is becoming less effective" and needs to be revised, Dr Dennis Maki, infectious diseases chief at the University of Wisconsin-Madison Hospitals and Clinics, told *NewsMax*.

A new study in the November 8, 2007 *New England Journal of Medicine*& by researchers at Oregon Health Science University [OHSU], supported by the United States Public Health Service, suggests that the schedule for vaccinating and revaccinating against diseases should be reevaluated and adjusted.

The study found that in many cases, the established duration of immunity for vaccines is greatly underestimated, which means that people are getting booster shots when their immunity levels do not require it and those antibody responses caused by viruses such as measles, mumps, and rubella remained at protective levels for several decades and in most cases, for life.

The research also reconfirmed a previous finding by [Mark] Slifka and his colleagues: that the duration of immunity after smallpox vaccination is much longer than previously thought. In that earlier study published in the journal *Nature Medicine* in 2003, these OHSU researchers observed surprisingly long-lived antiviral antibody responses but they were unable to measure the slow rate of decline.

The study indicates that the duration of immunity after smallpox vaccination is maintained with a calculated half-life of 92 years and that a person who has received the primary series of tetanus vaccine is likely to be protected for 3 decades.

## Over-Vaccination Can Cause Harm

Experts say we have allowed ourselves and our children to be overdosed through a culture dominated by industry marketing influence which has now become dangerously out of control and detrimental to our childrens health. "In the 21st century, it is unacceptable to be marketing medication to infants and children that may not work," Dr Steven Czinn, chair of the department of pediatrics at the University of Maryland School of Medicine, told Reuters on October 11, 2007.

In the November 19, 2007 *Huffington Post* article, "Over Medicated and Over-Vaccinated: The Unintended Consequence of Medicines Meant to Protect," Deirdre Imus asks, "Where are the conflict-free studies that prove giving infants and children 49 immunizations, most of them by age 5, are safe and effective?"

She points out that studies have provided evidence that the over-vaccination of dogs and cats can result in numerous maladies including cancer, skin and ear conditions, arthritis, allergies, diabetes, aggression, behavior problems and other immune system dysfunctions. "There is even a name for the conditions caused by animal over-vaccination, vaccinosis," she notes.

Ms Imus also points out that the mercury-containing preservative, thimerosal, used in vaccines for over 50 years, was removed from animal vaccines in 1992.

"Unfortunately for the kids," she writes, "it remained in childrens vaccines for another decade and remains in some vaccines like the influenza (25 micrograms) and tetanus vaccine (25 micrograms) today and in trace amounts (3 micrograms) in some immunizations."

She says most people do not realize that any liquid waste containing more than 200 parts per billion (ppb) mercury must be deposited at a hazardous waste site and that drinking water cannot exceed 2 ppb mercury.

"But when the influenza vaccines arrive and are injected into pregnant women and infants as young as six months, those vaccines contain 50,000 ppb mercury," Ms Imus notes.

"This amount of mercury is 250 times higher than hazardous waste," she notes, and according to EPA [Environmental Protection Agency] guidelines, this amount can only be considered safe if a person weighs 550 pounds. "Even trace amounts of mercury in vaccines can be anywhere from 600 to 2000 ppb," she warns.

On November 13, 2006, PutChildrenFirst.org, a parent-led organization advocating vaccine safety, issued a press release to announce the results of a survey conducted October 2730, 2006, by Zogby International of over 9,000 Americans to learn their plans for getting flu shots, their knowledge of its ingredients, and who they hold responsible for making sure vaccines are safe.

The survey showed that an overwhelming majority of Americans were unaware that most flu shots contain mercury and that they would refuse a shot with mercury. After learning that mercury is an ingredient, 74% of those polled said they were less likely to get a flu shot and 86% of parents said they were less likely to allow their child to get a shot.

Lisa Handley is a founding parent of PutChildrenFirst.org, whose son Jamison had an adverse reaction to a flu shot with mercury in 2003. "I know firsthand how life-changing a flu shot with mercury can be, since our son began his regression into autism after his flu shot," she states.

"With everything we know about the dangers of mercury and the havoc it can wreak on young, developing brains, there is no excuse for any vaccine to contain mercury," says Lyn Redwood, RN, MSN, President of SafeMinds, a nonprofit organization committed to ending mercury-induced neurological disorders.

"The survey reveals that Americans are overwhelmingly in the dark about what is in most flu shots," Ms Redwood stated in the press release.

---

*Forcing parents to inject poisonous concoctions into innocent, helpless children against their will is a gross violation of their most basic parental rights.*

---

"They do not want a known neurotoxin injected into their children, and they believe Congress and medical professionals must be more vigilant about keeping vaccines safe and mercury-free," she added.

## New Vaccines May Later Prove Unsafe

PutChildrenFirst also advises that two recent studies in leading medical journals admitted that limited data exists to support the effectiveness of flu vaccines. One study, in the *Journal of the American Medical Association*, noted that, "there is scant data on the efficacy and effectiveness of influenza vaccine in young children," the release notes.

According to Ms Imus, we are beginning to see prescribed vaccines, like the whole cell DPT [diphtheria, pertussis, and tetanus] and Rotavirus, which are later found to be unsafe.

"While physicians warn the public about the over use of antibiotics," she points out, "it is the physicians themselves that over-prescribed these antibiotics for every ailment under the sun."

"And like antibiotics," she writes, "every time a new vaccine was developed, it quickly found its way onto the immunization schedule along with the recommended booster shots."

"We are now reaping the unintended consequences of the overuse of these medical interventions," she states. "Instead of being healthier, we have a nation of very sick children."

Forcing parents to inject poisonous concoctions into innocent, helpless children against their will is a gross violation of their most basic parental rights.

# Does the Threat of Bioterrorism Warrant Mandatory Vaccination?

# Chapter Preface

Shortly after the terrorist attacks of September 11, 2001, brought down the World Trade Center in New York City and severely damaged the Pentagon in Washington, D.C., another ominous event occurred, stirring many Americans to the point of panic. Envelopes containing threatening letters along with a deadly strain of anthrax spores were sent to major news media and to several senators. Although the recipients were not harmed, a number of postal workers became seriously ill, as did some whose source of exposure was unknown. Five people died. In addition, whole buildings were contaminated for months and had to be evacuated. Despite long and intensive investigation by the Federal Bureau of Investigation (FBI) and others, the case has never been solved.

Americans feared that this was only the beginning of widespread bioterrorist attacks within the United States. For many weeks, anthrax made headlines. The postal service began irradiating mail; people were warned to be careful with mailed items and not to open anything received from an unknown source. Many bought duct tape and plastic sheeting to seal off their homes, though such measures would not have done any good unless it was known in advance when an attack was coming. In time, the excitement died down, but it spurred large increases in government funding for bioweapons research and preparedness. Among the new initiatives was the Bioshield Act, passed by Congress in 2004, which provides billions of dollars for the development and dissemination of new vaccines and drugs to protect against chemical, biological, radiological, and nuclear weapons.

The anthrax scare also led to much discussion of what should be done to protect civilians in case bioterrorist attacks do occur. A 2003 article by Wendy Orent in the *Los Angeles Times* argued, "Instead of giving the American people a real choice—access to existing vaccines against smallpox and anthrax—we've been offered duct tape and plastic sheeting and told to protect ourselves. . . . The one thing that would prepare us would be mass vaccination, and they're not even talking about that."

Smallpox was, and still is, a major worry. For centuries a much-feared disease, it has been totally eradicated throughout the world since 1977, when the last known case was found in Somalia. Since 1972, children are no longer vaccinated for it. Yet small amounts of smallpox-causing agents still exist in laboratories, and terrorists might be capable of securing these agents and reintroducing the virus into the public in the form of a terrorist attack. People were dismayed to learn that insufficient supplies of the smallpox vaccine was on hand—enough to protect no more than a fraction of the U.S. population. Eventually the government stockpiled enough for everyone. But there are now concerns about the safety of the vaccine, so a better one is being sought. Recent studies have also suggested that people vaccinated before 1972 may still be immune.

While some were upset because an anthrax vaccine was not offered to civilians within the United States, a major controversy arose over its use on military personnel. Many veterans of the 1991 Gulf War have suffered from an illness, commonly referred to as Gulf War Syndrome, that they believe was caused by this vaccine, so when it was made mandatory for troops serving in Afghanistan and Iraq, some refused it, often being punished or forced to leave the service for disobeying orders. Between 2001 and 2004, a significant number of the military who were given the vaccine did became ill. The government maintains that the anthrax vaccination was not the cause of their illnesses. However, in 2004 a federal judge ruled that it was illegal to force the vaccine on service members because it had not undergone the proper procedures for licensing, and for several years afterward such vaccination was voluntary. In 2005 the vaccine was officially approved by the FDA, and when in 2007 military authorities determined that not enough soldiers were accepting vaccination to protect the army in case of biowarfare, it again became compulsory. Although the U.S. government declares the vaccine to be safe, it acknowledges that an improved anthrax vaccine should be developed, and research toward that end is under way.

# Anthrax Vaccine Is Necessary to Protect Service Members

*Stephanie L. Carl*

*Stephanie L. Carl is a sergeant in the U.S. Army Seventeenth Public Affairs Detachment.*

Service members throughout the Central Command area of operations [in Afghanistan] have been receiving the anthrax vaccine.

Anthrax bacteria can be transmitted in various forms. The most concentrated and deadly form is the airborne type. For years, different countries and terrorist organizations have experimented with the production of anthrax as a biological weapon. Terrorists are not afraid to use it in that way, as evidenced by the anthrax cases that arose after Sept. 11, 2001.

Eleven Americans contracted inhalation anthrax. Of those 11, five succumbed to the deadly effects of the dreaded bacteria. Fortunately for the others, the symptoms appeared soon enough for antibiotics to be effective.

"Anthrax is dormant," said Staff Sgt. Christopher W. Butler, Headquarters and Headquarters Company, Combined Joint Task Force-76 [CJTF-76], senior medic. "It takes days for the symptoms to appear, and when they do they are similar to the symptoms of a cold or flu."

Butler is one of the medical professionals responsible for ensuring every service member in CJTF-76 is vaccinated against anthrax.

"There are no contraindications for the anthrax vaccine," said Spc. Brad Smith, Headquarters and Headquarters Company, medic.

That means everyone will receive the anthrax vaccine.

Stephanie L. Carl, "Anthrax Vaccine Protects Service Members," *Defend America* (now known as AmericaSupportsYou.mil), October 8, 2004.

## Vaccination Is Compulsory

"If someone comes to me and says they can't receive the vaccine, they have to have documentation from a doctor advising that they can't receive it."

There may be some cases of this, as some service members may have had an allergic reaction to the vaccine in the past. Others receiving the vaccine for the first time may have an allergic reaction. For those who do, it's important to seek medical attention.

"We're trained to handle allergic reactions to the vaccine," said Smith, who attended a 20-hour class that focused specifically on anthrax and the anthrax vaccine. However, not every reaction is allergic.

"Some people are bothered by the vaccine," said Col. Dallas W. Homas, surgeon. "Others have no symptoms at all. The most common symptoms are flu-like, along with a local reaction at the site (of the injection) with swelling."

Some side effects, like the flu-like symptoms, may last only a few days. Others, like the swelling, or even a lump, may last weeks. But these side effects don't outweigh the benefits of the vaccine.

---

*Just like you would wear [body armor] to protect against ballistics, we're going to give vaccines to protect against biological threats.*

---

"Anthrax is a nasty disease," said Smith. "It breaks down your immune system, and ultimately causes death."

While the inhalation form of anthrax is the most potent threat to service members serving in Afghanistan, there are other forms that are more prevalent. The vaccine also protects against the cutaneous and gastrointestinal forms, both endemic, or native, to Afghanistan.

Cutaneous anthrax is spread through direct contact with the bacteria. Any open wound or sore that comes in contact with anthrax can cause a person to become infected. This form is the easiest to treat, and can usually be cured with topical antibiotics.

A moderately more dangerous form, gastrointestinal anthrax is passed through food. In this form, the bacteria is ingested when a person eats contaminated food.

"All a soldier needs is a small cut and they can get anthrax," said Butler. "It can be transmitted through the blood or saliva."

This is especially important for service members who handle animals, especially sheep, on a regular basis. Additionally, service members who eat local food run the risk of contracting gastroinstestinal anthrax. Both of these forms can be easily protected against with the anthrax vaccine, along with the inhalation form, which can be used in a biological attack.

"Anthrax has been used against Americans in a weaponized form," said Homas. "It's a known threat, and we're an Army at war. We need to protect our combatants. Just like you would wear an (Interceptor Body Armor) to protect against ballistics, we're going to give vaccines to protect against biological threats."

# High-Risk Situations Justify Government Restrictions on Liberty

*Lawrence O. Gostin*

*Lawrence O. Gostin is associate dean, professor of law, and director of the Center for Law and the Public's Health at Georgetown University Law Center, Washington, D.C., and the author of several books.*

The government is engaged in a homeland security project to safeguard the population's health from potential terrorist attacks. This project is politically charged because it affords the state enhanced powers to restrict personal, and economic, liberties. Just as governmental powers relating to intelligence, law enforcement, and criminal justice curtail individual interests, so too do public health powers.

Disease control measures invade each of the major spheres of personal liberty: vaccination, physical examination, and medical treatment interfere with bodily integrity; disease surveillance, reporting, and data collection interfere with informational privacy; and isolation, quarantine, and criminal sanctions for risk-taking behavior interfere with liberty.... 

Homeland security is controversial because it places in conflict two sets of important values: the public's health and safety on the one hand and personal and economic liberties on the other. Some argue that we can have it both ways: protect the fullest expression of personal and economic liberties and attain the maximum degree of public health safety. Although security and liberty sometimes are harmonious, more often than not they collide. Advancing the common good fre-

Lawrence O. Gostin, "When Terrorism Threatens Health: How Far are Limitations on Personal and Economic Liberties Justified?" *Florida Law Review*, vol. 55, 2003, p. 1105. Reproduced by permission.

quently requires limitations on individual interests. Society therefore faces hard tradeoffs: individuals must forego some liberty to achieve a healthier and safer population; conversely, the government must permit some diminution of security to achieve a freer society. . . .

In response to the risk assessment . . . , government has proposed and enacted a set of powers that interfere with personal and proprietary interests: vaccination, treatment, and quarantine, as well as nuisance abatements and takings of private property. Commentators often claim that the state should not possess these and other liberty-limiting powers. [Later in this essay], I explain why asking whether the government should have liberty-limiting powers is the wrong question. The risk from bioterrorism can be stratified into three categories: significant risk, moderate risk, and negligible risk. The right question is, what powers should the state have to deal with each level of risk? Assuming the government's intervention is well targeted, the significant risk scenario unequivocally justifies the exercise of state power; arguably, a moderate level of risk could imbue the state with certain powers as well. Rather than inquiring whether liberty-limiting power is ever legitimate, commentators should ask what circumstances must exist to justify the exercise of authority. . . .

## Risk of Attack Warrants Limiting Liberty

Given that biological weapons are economical and relatively easy to develop, they pose a risk to the American public. The portability, inexpensiveness, lethality, and low risk of detection make developing a disease as an agent of terrorism attractive to groups determined to disrupt our way of life. The fact that multiple countries have already developed agents for bioterrorism is further evidence of their attractiveness. Adding to the risk is the fact that non-state actors have expressed the interest, if not yet the unfettered ability, to develop their own weapons. The risk has, in two cases, developed into a reality on American soil. Finally, the tipping point in a risk analysis is the severe harm to population health and the economy that would occur if a successful large-scale attack was carried out.

---

*Both liberty and economic freedom are central to our society. Yet, these freedoms have never been absolute. Both . . . need reconsideration in the new context of contemporary health threats.*

---

Given the evidence, it is reasonable to suggest that a threshold has been crossed justifying consideration of a liberty-limiting response to avert the risk or ameliorate the harm. Historically, infectious disease control has included measures that restrict personal privacy (e.g., surveillance), bodily integrity (e.g., vaccination and treatment), and liberty (e.g., quarantine). So too has government fettered the free exercise of property rights by, for example, seizure, closure, or destruction of private property or licensing and credentialing of professionals and institutions.

The fact that liberty-limiting powers are warranted still does not answer the question of how to make the hard tradeoffs between personal and economic liberty on the one hand, and national health and security on the other. In the context of the homeland security project, we face difficult decisions. Both liberty and economic freedom are central to our society. Yet, these freedoms have never been absolute. Both kinds of rights, civil and economic, need reconsideration in the new context of contemporary health threats.

## Proposed Governmental Powers

In response to the risk analysis just presented, federal and state governments have sought to introduce a variety of state powers designed to prevent, detect, and respond to bioterrorism. The powers needed to address bioterrorism relate to planning, surveillance, and restrictions on personal and proprietary freedoms. . . .

Planning provisions would put in place a process for thinking through each of the factors necessary for public health preparedness. A thoughtful strategic design must include: the actors (e.g., law enforcement, public health, and emergency management); decision-making processes; communication networks; and contingency plans such as procurement and deployment of supplies (e.g., vaccines, pharmaceuticals and hospital beds); licensing of health care professionals; destruction or seizure of dangerous property; and safe disposal of human remains.

Surveillance provisions would authorize measures for early identification of a public health emergency. The two principal forms of surveillance are passive and active. Passive surveillance includes case reporting—mandatory duties on health care professionals and laboratories to report patients with conditions of public health importance. Case reporting usually entails disclosure of a person's name and other identifying characteristics to the health department; consequently, there is an invasion of privacy.

Active surveillance includes powers to monitor health data to identify abnormal patterns suggestive of a public health emergency. For example, agencies are interested in unusual clusters of gastrointestinal or respiratory disease in emergency rooms or managed care organizations, inordinately large numbers of sales of anti-diarrhea medications in pharmacies, or sharp increases in absences from schools or workplaces. Active surveillance may, or may not, include personal identifiers. Although anonymous data are often sufficiently informative, in some cases health officials need personal identifiers to accurately track cases and avoid duplications. Surveillance, like intelligence in the criminal justice context, offers an early warning system essential for rapid identification and response to threats. At the same time, it invades a sphere of personal privacy by disclosing identifiable patient records to government health agencies.

Provisions for personal restrictions would follow traditional communicable disease control measures designed to secure prophylaxis against disease, reduced infectiousness, and/or behavioral change to prevent transmission. Classic interventions include: (1) vaccination to avert infection or ease its effects, which infringes on bodily integrity and perhaps freedom of conscience or religion; (2) testing and physical examination to identify persons exposed or infected, which implicate informational privacy interests; (3) medical treatment to alleviate symptoms and decrease infectiousness, which invades bodily integrity; and (4) quarantine to separate the ill from the healthy, which infringes on freedom of movement and association. . . .

Critics from both ends of the political spectrum stridently oppose the exercise of many of these powers. Liberty-limiting state power, they suggest, lacks justification in a liberal democracy, with its emphasis on individualism and free agency. More specifically, civil libertarians express a preference for personal freedoms of autonomous rights-bearing individuals—the right to privacy, bodily integrity, and free travel. Economic libertarians express a preference for economic freedoms of entrepreneurs—free enterprise, competitive markets, freedom to contract, and professional and business pursuits. Often, critics frame their arguments in absolute terms (the state ought not have power over individuals) rather than in relative terms (the state should have power only in clearly specified circumstances).

---

*The legitimacy of government action depends on the risk posed and the means used to diminish the risk.*

---

How seriously should we take these kinds of argument leveled against the introduction of state power? Is there any reason to conclude that [government powers such as curtailing nuisances, seizing hazardous materials, licensing professionals and health care facilities, and taking property for public uses] are irrational under prevailing theories of political philosophy or other forms of rigorous scholarly thought? The answer, of course, depends on the rationale for the exercise of power and the particular power sought. When deciding whether to intervene, the government must first assess the risk to the population, and then determine the means by which the risk can be managed. These two dimensions—the level of risk and the means adopted—are important in determining the legitimacy of the government action. . . .

## Justification Depends on Risk

The risk dimension and the means-ends dimension are interwoven. In any given case, the legitimacy of government action depends on the risk posed and the means used to diminish the risk. The state acts at its highest level of legitimacy when the risk is significant and the means well-targeted. The state acts at its lowest level of legitimacy when the risk is low and the means are ill-suited to achieve legitimate ends. It is important to stress that even in high-risk settings, means that exceed the scope of the threat or use public health as a pretext for discrimination are unacceptable.

---

*Individualism needs to be balanced against equally valid ideals of community safety.*

---

My principal argument is that the state's claim to possess appropriate liberty-limiting power is unmistakably valid for certain risk categories, assuming the proposed intervention is well targeted. In the significant risk hypothetical, . . . mainstream political theories support the exercise of appropriate authority. No hard choices are presented because the state restricts freedom of action to avert a tangible harm.

For the moderate risk category, the state's claim does present a hard problem, even if the governmental intervention is well-targeted. In the moderate risk hypothetical, critics have at least a *prima facie* [on first appearance] case that the state should not possess liberty-limiting power. Hard choices are required because this kind of case places in conflict alternative values—one preferring personal liberties and the other public goods. Here, I will suggest that, since two sets of values collide, it is necessary to take a position preferring one value over another or, at least, to weigh one value more heavily in constructing a public policy. Still, I will not accede to the prevalent liberal view of the unwavering primacy of the individual, but argue that individualism needs to be balanced against equally valid ideals of community safety.

For still other risk categories, the state's claim is almost certainly invalid. In the negligible risk or arbitrary action hypothetical, no liberty-limiting state power is permissible. This kind of intervention finds little support in serious political philosophical traditions because it violates basic tenets of liberalism (e.g., freedom and fairness) while failing to substantially advance any collective interest in health and security. Although illustrations of the exercise of authority against ethnic or religious groups can be found in American history, the courts often repudiate them as an abuse of power.

---

*It is important that the government has the authority to act quickly should a bioterrorist attack occur.*

---

It should be clear when examining these scenarios that commentators often ask the wrong question when inquiring about the appropriate scope of state authority in a public health emergency. They ask whether law should afford public health authorities the power to limit the freedoms of individuals and businesses. Indeed, the journals, newspapers and Internet are replete with claims that no legal authority should exist to vaccinate, treat, and quarantine individuals or to abate nuisances, seize property, or take property for public uses.

These arguments purport to apply, without differentiation, to all risk categories described above. However, . . . the significant risk scenario unequivocally justifies the exercise of appropriate state power; and the moderate risk category arguably justifies limits on individual interests. The argument that law ought not afford liberty-limiting powers to public health agencies finds no support in philosophical tradition, history, or constitutional law.

## Asking the Right Question

The central inquiry, then, is not whether government should have the power to act. It is overly simplified to suggest, as critics do, that liberty is always preferable to public health or that voluntarism is always preferable to coercion. Rather, the proper inquiry is under what circumstances power can be exercised— the standards, processes, and safeguards that fetter, but do not obviate, government power. By setting precise standards and requiring sound fact-finding procedures, the law seeks to differentiate between the valid and unjustified use of authority. . . .

The question faced is not whether the government should have liberty-limiting authority designed to cope with an attack, but what powers the state should have under what circumstances. American society prizes liberty and freedom, openness and tolerance; these values are part of the national identity and seem sometimes to rise to the level of inviolable tenets. These values, important in their own right, need to be balanced against equally valid values of population health and safety.

The task for society is to grant government power in a way that clearly separates the warranted (true risk reduction) from the unwarranted (negligible risk reduction or pretext for unfair treatment). That task is difficult enough even though most clear thinkers agree in principle about the legitimacy of state action in these contexts. What is still more difficult is setting justifiable boundaries for state action to address moderate risk situations where government cannot be sure of the precise parameters of the threat society faces. How can the law help assure that citizens' lives are secure, while preserving their values?

The answer to this question first requires a careful balance between individual and collective interests. The law must seriously consider authentic liberal claims to human dignity and tolerance of ethnic and religious minorities. At the same time, legal scholars should recognize that individual choices are shaped by the social context in which people live. The law must also take account of bona fide group interests, including a community's claim to a certain level of health, safety, and security. The law's objective, then, should be to take both private (personal freedom) and public (the social dimensions of human existence) interests seriously, recognizing that neither is dispensable.

## Conflicting Values

The problem with constructing legal standards and procedures for state action is that any formulation necessarily expresses a preference for one set of interests over another, even if government seeks to respect both. Setting the legal standard too high effectively thwarts legitimate collective interests because, in practice, government action is chilled if not blocked. Setting the standard too low results in the opposite error of excessive deference to state action. The law cannot calibrate precisely enough to split the difference exactly.

Society's preferred values will become transparent in the political process. My point, however, is that there is no reason, *a priori* [deduced before analysis], for choosing one set of values over the other. In particular, I do not concede that liberalism should be the *de fault* preference. "Rights," in other words, do not invariably trump common goods. Thus, if government can point to a moderate risk and proposes interventions that are reasonably well targeted and not unduly burdensome, the law should permit a sphere of state action. By doing so, each person bears a small burden (equitably distributed), but as members of a community all gain in the social exchange.

My refusal to cede to the primacy of individualism is animated by my concern for public safety in a health emergency. It is important that the government has the authority to act quickly should a bioterrorist attack occur. Quick action will be required on the part of both federal and local governments to minimize the impact of the attack and to protect the population. . . .

A successful framework would allow the government to act quickly in response to an emergency, but not allow individual liberties to be reduced to an unacceptable level. The best way to work toward this balance is to make use of traditionally successful mechanisms such as the democratic process, checks and balances, clear criteria for decision making, and judicial procedures designed to control the abuse of power by governmental agencies. In addition, the framework could adopt the modern concept of "shielding"—the governmental duty to engage the community in voluntary measures of self-protection as a "less restrictive alternative" to compulsion. This would involve government/community partnerships including effective state communication about health risks and self-preservation.

In truth, adoption of this framework will not guarantee an appropriate balance between liberty and security. The framework cannot assure that politically accountable government will act for the common good if liberalism remains the prevalent social value. The framework, however, is more likely to prevent government overreaching because it relies on a model of separation of powers. Yet, if the electorate gains confidence that checks on power will prevent governmental excesses, perhaps it will cede greater authority to the state to protect the public's health. That, at least, is the theory behind strong powers hedged with substantive and procedural safeguards.

# Service Members Should Not Be Ordered to Risk Damage to Their Health

*Bob Evans*

*Bob Evans is a reporter for the* Newport News Daily Press *in Virginia.*

Senior Airman Jessica Bond of Yorktown knew what she'd say when the time came, and she knew what would probably happen as a result. She'd already told her first sergeant what to expect, too.

So when she was ordered to take an anthrax vaccination [in 2004] at Seymour Johnson Air Force Base, N.C.—in preparation for deployment to Kuwait—she told him, "No, sir."

The next day, she was ordered to her commander's office, where she again refused and was busted from E-4 to E-1, the lowest enlisted rank. The commander-as-judge-and-jury is known in the military as an Article 15 nonjudicial punishment.

A week later, "they gave me an order to take it again. And again I refused." Another Article 15 followed, and the military began the process of kicking her out of the Air Force, after nearly four years of otherwise unblemished service. . . .

Bond wasn't the only person who refused to accept the risk of the vaccine before the voluntary program began. Pentagon officials say that from 2000 through 2004, 147 people left the military for refusing. Those numbers do not include people who were allowed to leave without formal punishment or to just not get the shot. Ronald Blanck, a former Army surgeon general, says about 300 left the service after refusing to take the shot before 2000.

Bob Evans, "'They Gave Me an Order . . . and I Refused,'" *Dailypress.com*, December 6, 2005. Reproduced by permission.

Bond says her reason for refusing was simple: When the orders came, she was the parent of a baby daughter and about to become a single parent because of a divorce. "If I got sick from that shot, who was going to take care of my daughter?" she asked.

## Convincing Illnesses Among Friends

Bond had spent months researching the effects and use of the anthrax shot since enlisting in 2000, less than a year after graduating from Tabb High School. She talked to a cousin who's a pharmacist and began reading the material that the Defense Department gives troops about the shot, she says.

The cousin advised caution, noting various ills attributed to the anthrax vaccine. And one statement from a military brochure stood out, she says: The vaccine, it said, had been given safely to veterinarians and veterinary students for decades.

"I called 50 different veterinary schools—every one I could find—and they said they didn't give it to any of their students. I figured that if they'd lie about that," she says of the military, "they'd lie about anything."

Bond also says she only had to look around the base for more evidence. Her former husband had a bad reaction, and so did several of her friends—especially the women, Bond says.

One woman went into anaphylactic shock within two hours of vaccination. That's a rare event involving an allergic reaction, in which a person's breathing becomes difficult and death can result. The woman had seizures and convulsions, and she was hospitalized for a week, Bond says.

Another female friend got the shot [in 1999] and has suffered severe joint pains, chronic fatigue and migraine headaches that regularly require hospitalization, Bond says.

Bond says that when she joined the military, "I was proud to be a part of something that was bigger than me" and gave the Air Force her obedience.

When her daughter was born two years later, that changed.

## Orders Meant Showdown on Vaccination

Bond's unit got orders to ship to the Middle East in late 2003. In January 2004, she was scheduled for her first anthrax shot.

At first, she says, her sergeant and others accused her of shirking her duty to stay home with her daughter.

"The deployment was no problem," Bond says. "I volunteered to go on a longer deployment, to Bosnia," which would have meant leaving her daughter with relatives. Bosnia isn't on the list of places where anthrax vaccination is prescribed.

Her bid for Bosnia was rejected, despite a need for her military contracting specialty, Bond says. Before her Article 15, Bond was provided a military lawyer, who told her that there was essentially no legal defense for refusing to take the anthrax shot. It's considered a lawful order. The Article 15 also meant that she couldn't appeal to a jury of her peers.

At one point, "my first sergeant asked me, 'Why would you think that your government would give you anything that's harmful?'" Bond says.

She says she listed a number of examples, including experiments involving exposure of troops to radiation in the 1940s and 1950s and use of Agent Orange plant-killer in Vietnam. All have been shown to cause health problems for thousands of troops. "He said, 'The military's changed,'" Bond recalls. She wasn't buying it.

After the two refusals, the sergeant and her commander pushed for a dishonorable discharge, which would make it difficult for her to get a decent job in civilian life. The general of her unit rejected that proposal, noting Bond's good conduct and achievement medals, commendations for job performance and otherwise unblemished record.

"I ended up getting a general discharge," Bond says. That still makes potential employers suspicious and cost her any G.I. Bill post-service benefits that she'd earned.

Bond says other members of her unit understand her choice. "They were very supportive," she says, and nearly all said they wished that they'd had the courage to refuse.

"Courage" isn't the word that Bond uses to describe her choice, however. "I'm no hero," she says. "The people over there, fighting that war, are the heroes."

# Mandatory Anthrax Vaccination Has Caused Many Serious Illnesses

*Greg Gordon*

*Greg Gordon is a Washington, D.C.–based investigative reporter for the McClatchy newspapers.*

En route home from the Persian Gulf on a military supply ship in 2003, merchant seaman James Francis and his mates got an ultimatum: Take anthrax and smallpox vaccinations or lose your jobs.

Francis' Seattle attorney, Russell Williams, described the shipboard scene the next day off the isle of Crete as: "Wham, bam. 'Get in line. Take your shots.'"

Within days of taking the two shots, Francis' feet began to tingle and burn. When he later took the second in a series of six anthrax shots, his health slid downhill. Since then, the 45-year-old messmate from Las Vegas has fought a rare nervous system disease known as Guillain-Barré Syndrome, along with chronic pain, pneumonia and a life-threatening blood clot.

Vaccine makers are immune from lawsuits, so Francis sued the government, winning what his lawyer calls a "substantial" settlement in December 2005. Others say Uncle Sam shelled out about $2 million.

## Mandatory Anthrax Vaccination Resumed

But Francis' success is unlikely to be duplicated by any soldier harmed in the massive anthrax inoculation program that's set to get under way in earnest early [in 2007]. Some 200,000

Greg Gordon, "Mandatory Anthrax Vaccinations Raise Concerns," Mcclatchydc.com, December 22, 2006. © Copyright 2006, The McClatchy Washington Bureau. Reproduced by permission.

troops, who unlike private employees are barred from suing the U.S. government, will be required to take the vaccine.

The Pentagon is reviving its mandatory anthrax vaccinations despite allegations that the shots have contributed to as many as 23 deaths and sickened hundreds, and perhaps thousands, of soldiers.

On [December 19, 2006], the Department of Health and Human Services [HHS] canceled an $877.5 million contract with California-based VaxGen. Inc. for what would have been a substitute anthrax vaccine. HHS said the company missed deadlines for beginning tests on humans.

That puts even more focus on the controversial, decades-old vaccine, which has been used to inoculate 1.5 million military personnel. The Pentagon has been rocked by criticism that it has failed to adequately track whether the shots have caused diseases. Indeed, as occurred with Francis, many soldiers are injected with several vaccines on the same day, making it harder to identify the cause of illnesses.

In 2004, lawyers for sick soldiers won a court injunction blocking the mandatory shots until the Food and Drug Administration [FDA] reviewed the license of Maryland-based vaccine manufacturer Emergent BioSolutions. In December 2005, the FDA declared the vaccine safe and restored the license.

But testimony from some military doctors undercuts that decision. Dr. Limone Collins, the medical director of the Vaccine Healthcare Center at the Army's Walter Reed Army Medical Center, testified that Francis had "a rare, vaccine-associated, neuro-immunological disease," according to court papers.

Dr. William Campbell, a neurologist at the center, said the dual vaccinations afflicted Francis with a Guillain-Barré variant in which the body's immune system attacks the nervous system.

In another case, the medical director of a Vaccine Healthcare Center at Lackland Air Force Base testified on behalf of

Nathan Torquato, a senior airman being court-martialed for using cocaine and methamphetamine to cope with muscle pain and chronic fatigue syndrome, which he blames on his anthrax shots. Helping Torquato win a lighter sentence, Dr. David Hrncir said it "appears that we are having higher numbers of people coming down with chronic fatigue syndrome as a result of this vaccine."

---

*Numerous public health experts believe [the anthrax vaccine] causes a range of problems, particularly among women and people prone to autoimmune diseases.*

---

Despite such testimony, Pentagon health chief William Winkenwerder announced on Oct. 16, [2006,] that safety questions had been resolved and that the shots would soon resume—the Pentagon now says in January—for troops deployed in the Middle East, Korea and other areas at high risk of a terrorist attack with germ weapons such as smallpox and anthrax.

## Government Says Vaccine Is Safe

Col. Randall Anderson, who runs the Military Vaccine Agency, said the Pentagon believes health risks from the anthrax vaccine "are equal to those of other vaccines" that cause illnesses in only a tiny percentage of those vaccinated.

Robert Burrows, Emergent's vice president of corporate communications, pronounced the vaccine—sold as Bio-Thrax—to be "safe and effective" and vetted "more than any in history."

But lawyers who succeeded in stalling the mandatory program in 2004 filed suit seeking a new injunction, alleging that the FDA manipulated data from a 1950s clinical study and circumvented its rules in licensing a vaccine that was modified multiple times.

Numerous public health experts believe BioThrax causes a range of problems, particularly among women and people prone to autoimmune diseases. They list Guillain-Barré, which can kill or paralyze; other neurological disorders; diabetes; arthritis; chronic fatigue syndrome; chronic muscle and joint pain; respiratory ailments; vision problems; memory loss; and depression.

The afflicted soldiers blame their government.

Retired Army Capt. B. David Hodge, 54, of Carlsbad, N.M., said he was serving as a chaplain when he and his Tennessee-based Army reserve unit were injected with half a dozen shots of anthrax vaccine at Fort Bragg, N.C., in 1990 before being deployed to Saudi Arabia.

Hodge said Army health care personnel refused at the time to identify the anthrax vaccine, instead calling it "Vaccine A." He said he burned with fever for several days and permanently lost feeling in his fingers. Now he fights an autoimmune disorder that's destroying his lungs. "I love my country," Hodge said. "It's my government I don't trust."

Retired Air Force Sgt. David Lyles, 32, of Mentor, Ohio, said he was injected with the shot in October 2003 at Youngstown Air Force Base. A few minutes later, Lyles said, he fell off a stool in the base's avionics shop from anaphylactic shock and hit his head on the cement floor. Lyles, who had always been athletic, said that he recovered from the concussion but that Guillain-Barré left him walking with a cane.

"If there is a problem with the vaccine, why subject people that are helping you defend what you believe in?" asked Lyles, who also said he's lost some of his short-term memory.

## Many Serious Reactions Reported

An FDA system that collects adverse reaction reports for all vaccines has recorded more than 4,700 reports related to anthrax shots over the last 16 years. The number of cases, the agency says, will "inevitably be underreported."

The FDA said it has received 23 reports of anthrax vaccine-related deaths, but has seen no proof that the shots were to blame. The FDA also couldn't readily estimate the number of serious illnesses associated with the vaccinations. In the past, it has estimated 500 cases.

---

*The Government Accountability Office said that the [anthrax] vaccine's long-term safety "has not been studied."*

---

Dr. Meryl Nass, an internist in Bar Harbor, Maine, who has specialized in anthrax vaccine-related illnesses, says the estimates of health problems are vastly understated.

Nass said she has treated more than 500 seriously ill patients and that at least 1,500 more have phoned or sent e-mails.

Defense Department officials say several studies, including analyses of soldiers' disability claims and of post-vaccination hospitalizations, debunk the health concerns. But as recently as May [2006], the Government Accountability Office said that the vaccine's long-term safety "has not been studied."

The Pentagon also draws criticism for giving anthrax shots with other vaccines. John Richardson, a retired Air Force pilot who has crusaded against the vaccine, charges that this is done "so they can hide which vaccine is causing the problem."

He cites the case of Rachel Lacy, a 22-year-old Army reservist who was awaiting deployment to the Persian Gulf in early 2003 when she received an anthrax shot and four other vaccinations at Fort McCoy, Wis.

A month later, she died of a pneumonia-like affliction at the Mayo Clinic in Rochester, Minn. The Pentagon called her death "a rare, tragic event that may have been related to vaccination," but said two expert medical panels couldn't identify any of the five vaccines as the culprit.

Pentagon spokeswoman Ann Ham said each reported death is similarly investigated, but none has been "causally associated with anthrax immunization alone." Anderson said a government immunization panel found no reason not to give vaccines together.

## Data Not Made Public

Much Pentagon data remain out of the public's reach, even though a Defense Medical Surveillance System tracks all illnesses among troops. After the National Academy of Sciences' Institute of Medicine found no proof of causal links between the vaccine and illnesses in 2002, but urged more research, the Pentagon stopped issuing quarterly analyses of BioThrax's effects. "There isn't a need for that," Anderson said.

David Geier, vice president of the Maryland-based Institute for Chronic Illnesses, and his father, Dr. Mark Geier, have analyzed the FDA's vaccine adverse reaction reports and published numerous articles on vaccine safety. David Geier said the reactions to BioThrax among healthy soldiers have been "many orders of magnitudes higher" than they've been for nearly all other civilian vaccines.

The Defense Department has said it's given the vaccine to an estimated 175,000 troops involved in the 1991 Gulf War, but said it didn't keep accurate records of who was inoculated.

A Department of Veterans Affairs advisory committee that investigated possible causes of Gulf War Syndrome, clusters of illnesses that afflicted some 200,000 war veterans, didn't rule out the anthrax vaccine as a possible cause, said Steve Robinson, a panel member and official of Veterans for America.

While Anderson said that more BioThrax studies are under way, Nass dismissed the Pentagon research as "epidemiological garbage."

For example, she cited a military study of vaccine links to optic neuritis that excluded troops who developed vision problems in their first 18 weeks in the military, even though many soldiers get their shots in boot camp. The study also omitted other soldiers not diagnosed within 18 weeks of vaccinations—shots given just before they were sent overseas where there were no ophthalmologists, she said.

The mandatory anthrax vaccine program has been beset with problems almost since deputy FDA commissioner Michael Friedman granted a 1997 Pentagon request to expand its use from protecting people against anthrax infection in skin wounds to shielding those who breathe it.

In 1998, FDA inspectors halted production until the vaccine's manufacturer, Michigan-based BioPort Corp. (now an Emergent subsidiary), corrected deficiencies. Its plant didn't reopen until 2002.

From 1998 to 2000, hundreds of active troops, reservists and National Guardsmen risked courts-martial by refusing to take anthrax shots for fear of health problems. Then the 2004 court injunction forced the Pentagon to shift to a voluntary program. About 50 percent of troops have refused the shots.

Vaccine critics note that both the VA [Veterans Administration] and the Pentagon have routinely paid disability benefits to soldiers who blame BioThrax for chronic illnesses, but they list the ailments as "service-connected" without mentioning the vaccine.

Virginia attorney Richard Stevens, who has handled a number of claims, said that way, "they always have plausible deniability."

# Compulsory Vaccination Against Bioterrorist Attacks Is Unjustified

*Tom Jefferson*

*Tom Jefferson is a physician and coordinator of the Cochrane Vaccines Field in Rome, Italy, an international nonprofit network aimed at promoting evidence-based health care practices around the world.*

Taken at face value the use of vaccines to prevent the effects of serious infections caused by a terrorist attack appears a sensible policy. In 1997 the United States Department of Defense initiated the compulsory anthrax vaccine immunisation programme to immunise 2.4 [million] military personnel. In December 2002 a similar programme, also involving civilians, was started against smallpox. In the first five and half months the Department of Defense administered 450,293 doses of smallpox vaccine. United States military personnel engaged in military operations in Iraq are immunised against smallpox and anthrax. As in any vaccination campaign, the incidence of the target disease and the characteristics of available vaccines are two key elements in decision making.

Naturally occurring anthrax is a rare disease. It occurs mostly in cutaneous form among those exposed to animal products (such as hides) and causes a rare and rapidly fatal—if untreated—respiratory illness (inhalation anthrax). Inhalation anthrax is the most likely form of the disease in the event of a terror attack as the use of anthrax spores for terror or warfare would probably follow dissemination at high concentration by aerial route. As smallpox was eradicated three decades ago, mass use of both vaccines in an antiterrorist role

Tom Jefferson, "Bioterrorism and Compulsory Vaccination," *British Medical Journal*, vol. 329, September 4, 2004, pp. 524–25. Copyright © 2004 British Medical Association. Reproduced by permission from the BMJ Publishing Group.

has an epidemiological justification only in the presence of a credible threat—the capability to produce and deliver large quantities of active agents to susceptible populations and the will to carry out such an action. Many suspected (and now know) that these conditions did not exist in the Iraq deployment and in the mountains of Afghanistan. The only recent recorded use of an infectious agent in a terrorist role (the anthrax mailing campaign in the United States) used bacteria that had been sourced from a US military establishment.

Both anthrax and smallpox vaccines have been in use for a long time, but there are few other similarities between them. The UK and US anthrax vaccines consist of alum precipitated cell-free filtrate of bacilli. The US vaccine (BioThrax), manufactured by the BioPort Corporation (Lansing, Michigan), is adsorbed onto aluminium hydroxide (so called adsorbed anthrax vaccine, or AVA). At present, in the USA VaxGen and Battelle are developing and testing a recombinant *Bacillus anthracis* vaccine candidate known as rPA102.

Evidence of the effectiveness of the predecessor vaccine to AVA relies on a 1950s study carried out by [P.S.] Brachman et al on 1249 adult workers in four tanneries in the north east of the United States. The study showed that the killed vaccine was 92.5% effective in preventing cases of cutaneous anthrax. Separate effectiveness estimates for cutaneous and inhalation forms were not reported, but the small numbers of inhalation anthrax found in the study left the authors unable to infer a protective benefit. This conclusion was based on the observation that during a concurrent epidemic no worker in the immunised arm of the study contracted the inhalation form of the disease, whereas four out of five infected workers in the placebo arm died. As the quality of reporting of the study is in keeping with its age, it is unclear whether random allocation to either arm did take place. Despite the authors' conclusion, the website of the anthrax vaccine immunisation programme of the Department of Defense claims proven protection against inhalation anthrax.

Workers in the intervention arm of the Brachman study had a higher rate of adverse events than in the placebo arm, but no large scale trial of AVA has ever been conducted. Live attenuated anthrax vaccines were tested in the then Soviet Union in the mid-70s and seemed effective against cutaneous anthrax.

---

*Investment in evaluation and in better and safer vaccines surely must be a requisite to have credible compulsory immunisation programmes involving huge numbers of adults of reproductive age.*

---

The current smallpox vaccinia virus vaccine (Dryvax) produced in the United Kingdom on behalf of the US government has remained virtually unchanged since the days of the eradication campaign. It is thought to have substantial potency when administered to previously unvaccinated adults, but the harm profile of the vaccine reflects its live attenuated content, with post-vaccination encephalitis [acute inflammation of the brain] occurring in around 2.9 cases per million primary vaccinated subjects. In one study of 450,293 inoculations up to 3% of vaccine recipients needed short term sick leave. One case of encephalitis and 37 cases of acute myopericarditis [inflammation of the muscular wall of the heart] developed after vaccination. No deaths were observed, and all patients recovered. Newer vaccines are currently being developed but are a long way from field testing. Trials of an improved version of Dryvax vaccine (ACAM2000) comparing the two vaccines head to head have recently been halted because of the occurrence of myocarditis in three of the 1132 volunteer participants. It is unclear in which of the arms and in what proportions the events took place.

The US effort to prevent the effects of infectious agents by vaccination seems to be based on an unproved threat and the availability of old vaccines for which relatively few controlled data exist. Whether a credible threat will provide a rationale for the use of current vaccines in future confrontations is not known. Intelligence or its interpretation by politicians has proved to be fallible. Attention has been paid to the surveillance of recipients of both types of vaccines, but such methods are no substitute for large, well designed field trials powered to detect both serological responses and rare but potentially important adverse events. Although field trials are expensive, logistically difficult to undertake, and unlikely to answer the issue of vaccine effectiveness during a terror attack, investment in evaluation and in better and safer vaccines surely must be a requisite to have credible compulsory immunisation programmes involving huge numbers of adults of reproductive age. Until such time, the choice of whether to be vaccinated or not should be left to the individual.

# CHAPTER 4

# What Are Some Future Uses for Vaccines?

# Chapter Preface

In the United States, most people take vaccination for granted as a routine aspect of children's health care, a standard precaution they consider wise though unlikely to be needed. A minority strongly contests this view, arguing that vaccines may do more harm than good. Neither the supporters nor the opponents of vaccination think much about the diseases it is intended to prevent, for those diseases were virtually wiped out in North America long before the present generation of children was born.

But in many other parts of the world, attitudes are different. In developing countries, millions of children die from infectious diseases each year. In the case of diseases for which vaccines exist, children still die from them because the people there cannot afford the vaccines, or they do not have access to them. Often the vaccines are not locally available, in part because the manufacturers make very little money on sales to poor countries. There are now organizations, such as the Global Alliance for Vaccines and Immunization (GAVI), that are working to provide vaccines to more children and adults in developing countries around the world. But not enough of the vaccines are being produced, and sometimes those designed for one geographical area do not work as well in others.

A still more serious situation involves diseases for which vaccines have not yet been developed. Malaria, for example, is a leading killer in many parts of the world; more than a million people a year die from it, 90 percent of whom are African children. So far, scientists have not succeeded in producing a vaccine that protects against it, although several are in the testing stage. Even more deaths in Africa—1.6 million in 2007—are caused by AIDS. An estimated 22 million people were living with HIV in Africa by the end of 2007, including 1.9 million newly infected people in that year alone. Besides these diseases, there are serious ones common elsewhere that few Americans have even heard of. Availability of vaccines to prevent them would save many lives.

Whereas some people in the United States are concerned about risks from vaccines and hold demonstrations to protest their mandatory use, citizens of other nations are more apt to protest the lack of them. In February 2008, cases of yellow fever were detected in Paraguay, the first in over thirty years. Some four thousand people blocked a highway for hours near the nation's capital city, Asunción, to demand a widespread vaccination program. The protest came after authorities said they had only one hundred thousand vaccine doses on hand. "We are asking the population to remain calm. The situation is under control," said Paraguay's public health minister, who was arranging for more vaccine to be flown in from other nations. According to the World Health Organization, an estimated thirty thousand people worldwide die annually from yellow fever, whose symptoms include fever, vomiting, jaundice, and bleeding from the mouth, nose, eyes, and stomach.

It is easy for people in rich countries to dismiss lack of vaccines as a minor issue compared to the many other troubles of today's world. In fact, most adults given the many other, more visible, problems they see each day. In fact, most adults in the United States, even those who obtain all recommended vaccines for their children, do not bother to be vaccinated against diseases for which they themselves are at risk. And yet globally, infectious disease is still a major problem. Moreover, in an era of global travel, it is all too possible that travelers might bring back diseases to areas from which they were once eradicated. Or an entirely new disease might emerge, as AIDS did as recently as the 1980s, leading to an equally disastrous worldwide epidemic. For these reasons, the production of vaccines and research leading to new ones will be important component of public health policy for a long time to come.

# Lives Could Be Saved by More Vaccination of Adolescents and Adults

*Steve Baragona*

*Steve Baragona is the communications and public affairs officer of the Infectious Diseases Society of America.*

New vaccines are available to make significant gains against cervical cancer deaths and debilitating pain from shingles, but infectious diseases experts warn that their full potential will not be realized without changes in the way vaccines for adults and adolescents are promoted, financed, and delivered in the United States.

The Infectious Diseases Society of America (IDSA) has released a new "blueprint for action" to prevent tens of thousands of deaths and illnesses caused by these and other diseases that can be avoided with a few simple shots. The blueprint is published in the June 15 [2007] issue of *Clinical Infectious Diseases*.

"We have done a great job in this country delivering vaccines to children, but we have done an awful job delivering vaccines to adults," said Neal A. Halsey, MD, professor at the Johns Hopkins University Bloomberg School of Public Health and chair of the IDSA Immunization Work Group that developed the policy blueprint.

For example, he points out that more than 90 percent of U.S. children are immunized against measles, mumps, whooping cough, hepatitis B, and other diseases. Rates of these diseases are at or near historic lows. In contrast, an estimated 175,000 adults are hospitalized and 6,000 die each year from

Steve Baragona, "Infectious Diseases Experts Issue Blueprint to Avert Thousands of Preventable Deaths," Infectious Diseases Society of America, June 15, 2007. Reproduced by permission.

pneumococcal pneumonia, but one in three adults over 65 has not been vaccinated against it. The Centers for Disease Control and Prevention (CDC) estimates that the cost of treating diseases that vaccines could prevent exceeds $10 billion annually.

## Cost Is a Problem

Cost is one factor in why adults do not get vaccinated—particularly the uninsured. "CDC has very effective systems for delivering vaccines to underserved children," said IDSA work group member Walter A. Orenstein, MD, associate director of the Emory Vaccine Center and former head of CDC's immunization program. "One of them is Section 317 of the Public Health Service Act, which helps state and local health departments provide vaccines to uninsured or underinsured patients—largely children—for free. Section 317 must now be expanded to catch underserved adults at highest risk."

While the program is cost-effective, expanding Section 317 will require a significant infusion of cash. Section 317's current $520 million budget will need an additional $170 million per year in order to cover all vaccines for uninsured adults, according to a recent CDC estimate. "It is essential that we provide adults access to these vaccines that save lives and prevent illnesses," Dr. Orenstein said, "but immunizing adults must not be done at the expense of children."

IDSA also is calling for all plans to cover all adult and adolescent vaccines recommended by CDC's Advisory Committee on Immunization Practices and to pay physicians adequately for office costs associated with immunization. Further, managed care plans should be measured in part on how well they immunize patients. Another principle supports exploring where immunization can appropriately take place outside the traditional office setting. Funding to support research into vaccines and vaccine delivery must be increased, and resources must be available to gather data on safety, efficacy, and usage.

---

*We have the tools to make dramatic improvements in adult and adolescent health, as we have for children.*

---

Physicians and patients also must be part of the solution, according to the IDSA blueprint. "Part of the problem lies with physicians, who are not accustomed to offering vaccines during routine visits with adult patients; and with patients, who are unaware the vaccines exist," said IDSA work group member William Schaffner, MD, chair of the Department of Preventive Health at Vanderbilt University. Doctors who serve adults must begin assessing adult immunization needs during routine preventive health care visits. Also, CDC should launch an education campaign to help improve awareness about vaccines and the illnesses they can prevent in adults.

"As health care workers, we set an example for our patients," Dr. Schaffner added. "We all must be fully immunized."

"We have the tools to make dramatic improvements in adult and adolescent health, as we have for children," said Andrew T. Pavia, MD, chair of IDSA's National and Global Public Health Committee, Chief of Pediatric Infectious Diseases at the University of Utah, and a member of the National Vaccine Advisory Committee. "IDSA's blueprint outlines the steps we must take to use these tools effectively. Now all we need is the will to take those steps."

# Measles Is a Major Cause of Death Among Unvaccinated Children in Africa

*William J. Moss*

*William J. Moss is an associate professor in the departments of Epidemiology, International Health, and Molecular Microbiology and Immunology at the Johns Hopkins University Bloomberg School of Public Health in Baltimore, Maryland.*

M easles has caused millions of deaths since its emergence thousands of years ago, probably as a zoonosis [a disease that can be passed from animals to humans]. Deaths from measles are due largely to an increased susceptibility to secondary bacterial and viral infections. This period of increased susceptibility lasts for several weeks to months after the onset of rash and is attributed to a prolonged state of immune suppression. Most deaths associated with measles are due to pneumonia. Although the global mortality from measles is falling, a new study in *PLoS Medicine* found that children in Nigeria, Niger, and Chad still recently faced unacceptably high mortality from measles, a largely preventable disease.

## Measles Case Fatality Ratios

Measles case fatality ratios vary depending upon the average age of infection, the nutritional status of the population, measles vaccine coverage, and access to health care. In developed countries, less than one in 1,000 children with measles die. But in endemic areas in sub-Saharan Africa, the measles case fatality ratio often ranges from 5%–10%.

Measles is a major cause of child death in refugee camps and in internally displaced populations, and case fatality ratios

William J. Moss, "Measles Still Has a Devastating Impact in Unvaccinated Populations," *PLoS Medicine*, vol. 4, January 2007, pp. 9–10. Reproduced by permission.

in children in complex emergencies have been as high as 20%–30%. For example, during a famine in Ethiopia, measles alone or in combination with wasting accounted for 22% of 159 deaths among children younger than five years of age, and 17% of 72 deaths among children aged five to 14 years.

The risk of death following measles is highest at extremes of age and in those with underlying malnutrition and vitamin A deficiency. Exposure to an index case within the household may result in more severe disease, perhaps because of transmission of a larger inoculum of virus.

---

*Vaccinated children, should they develop disease after exposure, have less severe disease and significantly lower mortality rates.*

---

Interestingly, data suggest that measles mortality may be higher in girls. Among persons of different ages and across different regions (primarily in the Americas and Europe), measles mortality in girls was estimated to be 5% higher than in boys. Supporting the hypothesis of biological differences in the response to measles virus between boys and girls was the observation that girls were more likely than boys to have delayed mortality following receipt of high-titer measles vaccine.

## Measles Vaccination

Vaccinated children, should they develop disease after exposure, have less severe disease and significantly lower mortality rates. Vaccination programs, by increasing the average age of infection, shift the burden of disease out of the age group with the highest case fatality (infancy), further reducing measles mortality.

Several attenuated measles vaccines are available worldwide, either as single-virus vaccines or in combination with other vaccine viruses (commonly rubella and mumps). The proportion of children who develop protective antibody levels following measles vaccination depends on the presence of inhibitory maternal antibodies and the immunological maturity of the vaccine recipient, as well as the dose and strain of vaccine virus. About 85% of children develop protective antibody levels when the measles vaccine is administered at nine months of age, and 90%–95% have a protective antibody response after vaccination at 12 months of age. Most children who do not respond to a first dose of measles vaccine will respond to a second dose at an older age. The duration of protective antibody levels following measles vaccination is more variable and shorter than that acquired through infection with wild-type measles virus, with an estimated 5% of children losing protective antibody levels 10 to 15 years after vaccination.

---

*Remarkable progress in reducing measles incidence and mortality has been made in parts of sub-Saharan Africa as a consequence of increasing measles vaccine coverage.*

---

## Global Decline in Measles Mortality

Prior to the development and widespread use of measles vaccines, measles was estimated to result in 5 to 8 million deaths annually. The decline in mortality from measles in developed countries was associated with economic development, improved nutritional status and supportive care, and antibiotic therapy for secondary bacterial pneumonia, as well as the widespread use of measles vaccine.

In 2003, the World Health Assembly endorsed a resolution urging member countries to reduce the number of deaths attributed to measles by 50% by the end of 2005 compared with 1999 estimates, a target that is likely to have been met. Overall global measles mortality in 2004 was estimated to be 454,000 deaths (uncertainty bounds 329,000 and 596,000 deaths), a 48% decrease from 1999. Following this success, the global measles control goal now is to reduce the annual number of measles deaths by 90% by 2010 compared to the estimated number in 2000.

Remarkable progress in reducing measles incidence and mortality has been made in parts of sub-Saharan Africa as a consequence of increasing measles vaccine coverage, provision of a second opportunity for measles vaccination through supplementary immunization activities, improved case management, and enhanced surveillance with laboratory confirmation of measles cases. This accelerated measles control strategy began in 2001 with the support of the Global Alliance for Vaccines and Immunization and the Measles Initiative.

## Recent Outbreaks

How successful has this accelerated measles control strategy been? One measure of success is the recent demonstration of measles outbreaks in countries where these strategies had *not* been implemented.

The new study in *PLoS Medicine*, by Rebecca Grais and colleagues, provides estimates of measles attack rates and age-specific case fatality ratios during large measles outbreaks in Niger, Chad, and Nigeria during 2004–2005. The authors conducted retrospective household surveys in one neighborhood of each affected area at a time when the measles outbreak was subsiding, encompassing a total population surveyed of over 64,000 individuals. Routine measles vaccine coverage rates were low, supplementary immunization activities had not yet been conducted, access to health care was poor, and responses to the outbreaks were delayed, an epidemiological situation conducive to the rapid spread of measles virus with high rates of morbidity and mortality.

Almost 3,200 cases of measles were identified in the study areas with age-specific attack rates of 17% to 24% in children less than five years of age. About two-thirds of persons with measles developed respiratory complications and diarrhea.

The case fatality ratio ranged from 2.8% to 7% and was highest in children less than five years of age. Most deaths occurred in unvaccinated children and at home. In rural Nigeria the risk of death was higher in girls than boys.

Although subject to potential recall and misclassification biases, the estimates of morbidity and mortality during these large outbreaks of measles in Niger, Chad, and Nigeria are consistent with prior estimates obtained in similar epidemiological settings. The population surveyed was large and the non-participation rate was small.

## Implications of the Study

At a time of accelerated measles control in sub-Saharan Africa, these estimates serve as a reminder of the devastating impact measles can have in unvaccinated populations. During the outbreak, half of all deaths in children less than five years of age were attributed to measles. Prompt recognition and response to measles outbreaks, in addition to appropriate case management, is critical to reducing measles morbidity and mortality and preventing further transmission of measles virus.

These outbreaks also should serve as a reminder to communities in resource-rich countries of the importance of measles vaccination and the potential for imported measles cases to spark outbreaks in unvaccinated communities. Following the reported outbreaks in Niger, Chad, and Nigeria, accelerated measles control strategies were implemented in the affected areas, including mass measles vaccination campaigns. However, only sustained efforts to maintain high coverage rates of the routine first dose of measles vaccine, coupled with periodic opportunities for a second dose, will achieve the level of population immunity required to avert the unacceptably high morbidity and mortality rates that result from measles epidemics in susceptible populations.

# Children Infected with HIV Need Access to Pneumonia Vaccine

*Orin Levine and Paul Zeitz*

*Orin Levine is a Johns Hopkins University professor and execu-
tive director of the PneumoADIP program of the Global Alliance
for Vaccines and Immunization (GAVI), an organization focused
on a global effort to create greater access to the benefits of immunization. Paul Zeitz, a doctor, is executive director of the Global AIDS Alliance.*

Today, from Haiti to Mozambique to Cambodia, we're better than ever at reaching people with life-saving treatments for HIV/AIDS, even in the poorest places in the world.
But every day, 6,800 people are newly infected and nearly
6,000 more die of the disease.

With an AIDS vaccine still far off, reducing this toll requires not only more HIV-specific treatment, prevention and
care, including for children, but also prevention of life-
threatening infections—of which HIV-positive people are at
particularly high risk because of weakened immune systems—
pneumonia, for example.

The leading cause of pneumonia, a bacterium called the
pneumococcus, kills 1.6 million people a year, mostly in Africa
and Asia and mostly children.

## HIV-Positive Kids Vulnerable to Pneumonia

Kids Infected with HIV are especially vulnerable to serious
pneumococcal infections like pneumonia and meningitis, with
up to 40 times higher risk than other children. And once
they're sick, HIV-positive children are far more likely to die

Orin Levine and Paul Zeitz, "Poor Children Infected with HIV Need Access to Vaccines," Philly.com, December 13, 2007. Reproduced by permission.

from pneumococcal disease, especially when, as is frequently the case, they are not getting appropriate AIDS medication.

Unlike many other crises afflicting poor countries, however, this one is largely preventable. Children can be protected from these diseases for a lifetime by a simple vaccine. In rich countries like the United States, they are.

In poor countries, many of which have the higher rates of HIV in the world and account for 90 percent of all childhood pneumococcal deaths globally, the impact of pneumococcal vaccines would be especially great.

---

*Distribution of a pneumococcal vaccine to all children throughout the developing world could save the lives of 5.4 million by 2030.*

---

A new study published in the *Lancet* shows that pneumococcal vaccination is a crucial and effective lifesaver for HIV-infected children, whose greatly increased risk of infection makes them the biggest beneficiaries of the vaccine.

Unfortunately, the vaccine is not yet available in the developing world.

## Vaccines Could Save Many

There is growing recognition, starting with the tide of global response to the AIDS pandemic, that it is morally unacceptable for people in poor countries to die of a disease from which people in rich countries are protected.

The earliest AIDS activists in the United States and Europe deserve great credit for bringing this injustice to light. Having persuaded their neighbors that ignoring the West's simmering AIDS crisis was short-sighted and inhumane, they turned their attention to the epidemic's horrific toll in Africa and the rising risks to Asia and Latin America. If people are resolved to ease the anguish of AIDS in San Francisco and New York, the activists argued, they should be just as determined to do so in Nairobi and Bangkok.

These days, few people are willing to accept that geography should determine who lives and who dies. Cost-effective interventions such as vaccines can level the playing field and are one of the best investments in global health.

Pressured by activists, the United States and other wealthy nations have agreed that everyone in the world should have access to AIDS prevention, treatment and care by 2010. Donor nations should expand that commitment to other life-saving interventions, including pneumococcal vaccination for children.

Distribution of a pneumococcal vaccine to all children throughout the developing world could save the lives of 5.4 million by 2030.

With continued support and cooperation, that target will be met. The Global Alliance for Vaccines and Immunizations (GAVI), along with key donors such as the Bill and Melinda Gates Foundation, Italy, the United Kingdom, Norway, Russia and Canada, is putting in place a $1.5 billion fund to pay for pneumococcal vaccinations around the world. The effort is great news for children in developing countries.

The same kind of commitment will be needed to finance vaccines for malaria and tuberculosis, currently in trials and expected to be available in a matter of years. And such an advance commitment, we trust, will one day help make an effective AIDS vaccine available in the developing world.

Until then, the pneumococcal vaccine will play a major role in protecting the world's children. It offers real hope for curbing the damage HIV can do to some very vulnerable kids and for saving many lives in the years ahead.

# More Women Should Be Enrolled in HIV Preventive Vaccine Trials

*Edward Mills, Stephanie Nixon, Sonal Singh, Sonam Dolma, Anjali Nayyar, and Sushma Kapoor.*

*Six authors collaborated on the following article: Edward Mills, who is director of the Centre for International Health and Human Rights Studies at McMaster University in Canada; Stephanie Nixon, who is an AIDS researcher at the University of KwaZulu-Natal in South Africa; Sonal Singh, who teaches in the Department of Medicine at Wake Forest University in North Carolina; Sonam Dolma, who is a fellow in the department of political science at York University in Canada; Anjali Nayyar, who is vice president of Country and Regional Programmes at the International AIDS Vaccine Initiative in New York; and Sushma Kapoor, who is consultant gender advisor to the International AIDS Vaccine Initiative in New York.*

With almost 5 million new HIV infections and 3 million deaths from AIDS occurring every year worldwide, the development of a safe, effective, and accessible HIV vaccine has become one of the most urgent global public health needs. The United Nations estimates that 17.5 million women between the ages of 15 and 49 years are living with HIV, accounting for nearly half of the 40.3 million infections worldwide. These figures reveal the increasingly female face of AIDS.

As with many diseases, women in developing countries are particularly vulnerable to HIV. Poverty—and women's necessary reliance on men for economic subsistence—may force some women to exchange sex for money or material favors. Women in some cultures lack access to information on pro-

Edward Mills, Stephanie Nixon, Sonal Singh, Sonam Dolma, Anjali Nayyar, and Sushma Kapoor, "Enrolling Women into HIV Preventive Vaccine Trials: An Ethical Imperative but a Logistical Challenge," *PLoS Medicine*, vol. 3, March 2006, pp. 308–10. Reproduced by permission.

tection from and treatment of sexually transmitted infections. There may be societal pressures for women to have children, thereby affecting their use of contraception. Also, in many settings, women and girls lack the ability to negotiate safe sex or demand fidelity in a relationship. For most women in these situations, it is not their own behavior but the behavior of their partners that puts the women at risk of sexually transmitted infections, including HIV. The possibility of a preventive HIV vaccine, therefore, holds tremendous promise for women.

Despite the epidemiologic reality, women have had minimal participation in HIV vaccine trials. To develop HIV vaccines with regional efficacy, it is important to identify and characterize the viruses that are transmitted, in particular to individuals living in areas and conditions of high incidence. Enrolling women in HIV vaccine trials represents an important challenge that must be fulfilled in order to conduct ethical, valid, and generalizable trials.

## Women's Concerns About Trials

Efforts to enroll and retain women in trials begin by recognizing that their expectations and requirements for participation may be different from those of men. Women may lack the decision-making freedom to participate in a trial, especially a trial that addresses sexual behavior. They may be burdened with childcare and a lack of transportation. For women with children, participation is often limited by having to attend one of the few trial sites that offer childcare. Indeed, trials requiring that pregnancy and breast-feeding be avoided may place undue stress upon participants in cultures that place value on women's fertility.

Some cultural barriers identified in the recent HIV vaccine candidate trial in Kenya included women's belief that a woman of childbearing age who uses contraceptives is giving her husband an excuse to look for another woman with whom to bear children. On the other hand, men believed that child-bearing was a way of keeping women from infidelity. Condoms, which were recommended for use during the trial, were perceived as instruments to promote extramarital relationships.

To identify and tackle such barriers, trial staff require gender-specific guidance and training, while recruitment materials should be geared toward both sexes. Supplying trial centers with counselors and staff who are sensitive to gender, class, and cultural barriers may improve women's access to HIV vaccine trials. Allowing flexible clinic hours to meet the specific needs of patients is one of many pragmatic solutions resulting from such sensitivity training.

## Fear of Adverse Effects

Participants in HIV vaccine trials often fear that they will become HIV-positive through participation, either through infection from the vaccine or from antibodies produced by the vaccine, which would test positive in some test kits. A specific female concern is the unknown effects on future pregnancies. This fear is compounded by the concern among women that they may be unable to travel or to attain insurance or employment if they test positive as a result of the vaccine.

*Conducting valid and generalizable HIV vaccine trials requires the equitable inclusion of women.*

At least some of these fears could be allayed by community participation in the form of community advisory boards and the engagement of local community representatives in designing educational materials to educate the medical community and population at large.

## Informed Consent

Obtaining consent is a further challenge in some female populations, as women in poorer countries often lack formal education and may not understand the uncertainty that exists within clinical trials (the therapeutic fallacy). The principle of informed consent is that consent is freely given, without coercion from trialists or the local community. Therefore, all trial-related information should be presented in the local language, and should address varying levels of education in both written and oral presentation so that participants fully understand their rights, risks, and potential benefits. Participants need to be questioned on their understanding of the trial process. The informed-consent sheets should be prepared in consultation with the community advisory board and piloted within the target community to ensure gender and social sensitivity.

## Confidentiality

The International AIDS Vaccine Initiative has elucidated the basic requirements of the physical setting required of trial sites. However, ensuring confidentiality is a challenge in centres that are in public view. For women, any breach of confidentiality can lead to increased discrimination and harassment. Women may be subjected to violence or abandonment by their male partners or to discrimination from their employers if they are seen entering trial centres. Other implications include the refusal of sex as a result of a woman's presumed risky lifestyle. Safeguards to maintain confidentiality must therefore be in place. Diagnostic tests should only be disclosed to the participant, and supportive counseling should be provided before and after the tests, regardless of the frequency of HIV tests required.

## Barriers Faced by Sex Workers

Sex workers, due to the nature of their work, experience additional concerns. In addition to difficulties related to informed consent, confidentiality, and fear of infection, sex workers may experience continual exposure to coarse client interactions and violence. Sex workers thus require services that address both domestic abuse and client-related violence. They should also receive educational sessions on common myths about safe sex, including false information that may be given to them by their employers or partners. Education efforts regarding safe sex should not just involve the trial participants but also their clientele. To accomplish this, the promotion of condom use and safe sex in the commercial sex districts and bars frequented by the clientele is required. Studies have shown that many women require permission from their partners and employers to undergo HIV testing, at times at the risk of violence. Education aimed at sex workers' partners and employers could make this process more socially acceptable.

## Benefits of Participation

Considering the social risks of HIV vaccine trial participation, the immediate benefits to women are small; efforts to recognize their participation begin by appreciating the value of their role. The benefits that might arise from participation include the potential that HIV education may reduce the risk of infection and that participants might receive health care and contraceptive advice that would not normally be provided in communities where health services are limited. We should, however, recognize that despite education on safer sex for women, safe sex is most often determined by their partners' behavior.

Conducting valid and generalizable HIV vaccine trials requires the equitable inclusion of women. Barriers for participation of women are often systematically different from barriers for men, since the barriers to women stem from their often lower social status and lack of decision-making rights. Due to the number of different HIV clades [group descended from a single ancestor], trials need to be conducted in a variety of cultures and classes. Although differences in women's rights exist between varying cultures, most often in settings with high HIV prevalence, women suffer from a lack of empowerment in health and the possibility of violence or social discrimination for being involved with people living with HIV/AIDS or participating in a trial of this unmentionable subject.

In order to conduct clinically meaningful subgroup analyses, a large enough sample of the planned subgroup must be available, with adequate power to detect an effect. To ensure adequate power within the trial participants, the participants must be at risk of infection. Thus, enrolling females at high risk in HIV-endemic regions allows room to make important clinical inferences, but puts these individuals in potentially risky situations.

Recommendations to support gender recognition and sensitivity are often provided for staff allied to the trial (such as coordinating clinic staff). Efforts to create a specific, gender-sensitive, and informed consent process are undermined if the manner with which the consent is presented or obtained is not respectful and inclusive of the target community. Gender advisors and community advisory boards made up of key informants from the risk groups can inform education efforts aimed at potential trial participants. We acknowledge that cultural differences in women's rights can be extreme, and that in-depth knowledge of the community, where the trial is being conducted, is imperative to understanding barriers to participation. . . .

Recruitment efforts to include at-risk women in HIV vaccine efficacy trials are diverse, and require active involvement of community agencies. Successfully retaining these women over time presents ongoing challenges that relate to the trial validity, which will need to be addressed to ensure women's involvement in future trials. The AIDS Community Health Initiative Enroute to a Vaccine Effort (Project ACHIEVE), a vaccine preparedness study in New York City's South Bronx area, successfully retained 92% of women enrolled after one year. Similar retention rates have been replicated in HIV vaccine trials with similar cohorts of women in New York. Concerns about retaining hard-to-reach populations should not cause the exclusion of high-risk women from HIV vaccine and other prevention trials.

---

*Enrolling women in HIV vaccine trials worldwide represents an important challenge.*

---

The recent cessation of the tenofovir [an antiretroviral drug used to treat HIV] pre-exposure prophylaxis [preventive treatment] trials in sex workers in Cambodia and Cameroon demonstrates the difficulties of ensuring the rights of the enrolled participants. The trials closed early due to widespread complaints that the participant communities had not been involved in the planning of the trials. The events that halted the trials exemplify the need to involve the target groups in the planning of prevention trials.

## Researchers as Human Rights Advocates

[Edward Mills and Sonal Singh] recently advocated for the development of standards for community advisory boards, such as exist for ethical review committees, so that efforts to engage the target populations will transcend tokenism. We recognize that this concept will be new for many clinical trialists. We believe that researchers, by the nature of their work, should be advocates for the rights and protection of trial participants, and in communities and countries where the rights of the participants are threatened, researchers should determine if it is appropriate to engage in research there and seek assistance from human rights monitors when there is uncertainty. The development of trial protocols needs to consider accounts of violence and human rights violations, and develop a strategy for improving conditions for individuals or communities affected.

Today's AIDS research uses technologies that may be exciting from a scientific standpoint but are challenging when we consider the risks participants may incur by participation. Many high-risk communities are ready to assist in research, but researchers must be prepared to assist the communities beyond the trial's duration and ensure that local standards of medical care are improved through the research itself and also through the presence of researchers who advocate on participants' behalf.

Enrolling women in HIV vaccine trials worldwide represents an important challenge. Ensuring that the rights and needs of this population are respected and met requires community involvement and representation. Researchers must be sensitive to the needs of high-risk and vulnerable groups, from the initial stages of the trial through to unforeseen future events. By implementing strategies to enroll and protect the high-risk and vulnerable participants, we can appreciate the enormous contributions they are making to science.

# Experimental AIDS Vaccines Have Not Been Successful

*John Lauerman*

*John Lauerman is a reporter for the Bloomberg News service.*

The failure of Merck & Co.'s experimental AIDS vaccine may put an end to HIV prevention projects by the U.S. and GeoVax Labs Inc.

Merck halted a study, called STEP, in September [2007] after an unanticipated finding: people who got the vaccine were more likely to contract HIV than those who didn't. The result . . . has stalled human studies of similar vaccines, including one from the U.S. government that shares features with Merck's product.

The Merck vaccine was the most advanced of several preventatives against HIV, the AIDS-causing virus infecting more than 33 million people worldwide. Now, Anthony Fauci, the U.S. government's top infectious disease scientist, is waiting for more data from Merck and an international network of HIV researchers to determine whether the government's leading vaccine candidate, called VRC, will be safe enough to test.

"No final decision has been made on whether the trial is going to go forward," Fauci said in a telephone interview. "If it does, it will probably be a modified, truncated version" of earlier plans.

Scientists say the Merck fallout may set back vaccine research for years, and the other vaccines aren't as promising.

"There's a lot of disappointment," said John Bartlett, a Johns Hopkins University HIV researcher, in a telephone interview. "Prevention is the biggest failure in the field, I think everyone agrees."

## Features in Common

The government vaccine contains a cold virus made by Gaithersburg, Maryland-based GenVec Inc. and a DNA vaccine made by San Diego-based Vical Inc. It has at least two features in common with Merck's. First, while most vaccines spur the body to make protective proteins called antibodies, the experimental AIDS shots stimulate protective T-cells, white cells the immune system uses to attack viruses.

Both vaccines also were built using the cold virus, called adenovirus-5. Proteins that can trigger a protective immune system reaction to HIV are packaged within the virus that delivers them throughout the body. Atlanta-based GeoVax is also testing a T-cell vaccine that contains a virus.

AIDS researchers are concerned because, in the Merck study, the people most likely to become infected with HIV were those who had high levels of immunity to the cold virus before the test began. If the U.S. trial goes ahead, it should probably enroll less than half the 8,000 or more people originally proposed, and exclude anyone with immunity to the cold virus, government science advisors said at a meeting in Potomac, Maryland, in December [2007] to discuss the vaccine's fate.

---

*You can't just say globally that T-cell vaccines won't protect against HIV. . . . We know that T-cells are an important component of protection and they will continue to be.*

---

Eight government-funded studies of vaccines against HIV, malaria and Ebola virus were halted or put on hold after the Merck results. The International AIDS Vaccine Initiative, based in New York, has stepped up efforts to find a way to prevent the disease that doesn't depend on triggering protective T-cells. . . .

Researchers are expected to give an in-depth analysis of data from the STEP study, which Merck and the HIV Vaccine Trials Network ran together. The data may tell Fauci whether the cold virus itself raised the risk of infection.

"What was the mechanism of why they had a greater incidence of infection and what's the relationship?" he said. "It's going to be discussed, and it's going to be of great interest."

At the December meeting of the government advisory group, the AIDS Vaccine Research Subcommittee, most researchers said they were in favor of going ahead with testing vaccines related to Merck's. The government's shot is sufficiently different from Merck's to be worth testing, said Gary Nabel, director of the Vaccine Research Center in Bethesda, Maryland, where the preventive was developed.

"We're not giving up, but we need to be intelligent about the approach," he said at the meeting. "We need to move forward in a way that's constructive."

## Worth the Risk

Salim Abdool Karim, a vaccine researcher at the University of KwaZulu-Natal in South Africa, where the VRC may be tested, said the information to be gained in the test is worth the potential risk. A small trial would establish whether the vaccine is safe and provokes an immune response to HIV, he said.

"Given that we know so much about what this vaccine does in animals, it would be useful to see what it can do in people," he said in a telephone interview. "I don't think the T-cell vaccines are dead because of [the Merck failure]."

GeoVax's vaccine contains a virus called poxvirus. The product has significant differences from the Merck vaccine, and has given good results in animal tests, said Harriett Robinson, chief scientific officer and developer of the vaccine.

"You can't just say globally that T-cell vaccines won't protect against HIV," she said in a telephone interview. "We know that T-cells are an important component of protection and they will continue to be."

GeoVax expects to enter the second of three phases of human testing of its vaccine in mid-2008. The three levels of testing are required for sale in the U.S.

Researchers from Whitehouse Station, New Jersey–based Merck may also have more information on whether other viruses made people in the vaccinated group more vulnerable to infection, said Michael Robertson, the company's director of HIV vaccines clinical research. For example, the herpes virus has been shown to increase the risk that people exposed to HIV will become infected.

"We think that work will be very interesting," he said at the Maryland meeting. "We don't have anything that will shed any light on this so far."

## Phambili Trial

Researchers also want results from a second trial of the Merck vaccine that was under way in South Africa when the STEP results were released. The second trial, called Phambili, was stopped early, and patients who got the Merck vaccine were told they might be at higher risk of HIV infection.

The Phambili researchers had hoped to reveal . . . whether more vaccinated than unvaccinated people became infected. . . . Study leader Glenda Gray said she believes they will follow the same pattern as the STEP trial.

"We expect to see similar figures," said Gray, director of the Perinatal HIV Research Unit at Chris Hani Baragwanath Hospital in Soweto, in a telephone interview. "I think everyone would be surprised if it was different."

# A Malaria Vaccine Is Desperately Needed in Africa

## Michael Finkel

*Michael Finkel is a nationally known journalist who has contributed to* Atlantic Monthly, Rolling Stone, Esquire, *and* National Geographic.

It begins with a bite, a painless bite.

The mosquito comes in the night, alights on an exposed patch of flesh, and assumes the hunched, head-lowered posture of a sprinter in the starting blocks. Then she plunges her stiletto mouth-parts into the skin.

The mosquito has long, filament-thin legs and dappled wings; she's of the genus *Anopheles*, the only insect capable of harboring the human malaria parasite. And she's definitely a she: Male mosquitoes have no interest in blood, while females depend on protein-rich hemoglobin to nourish their eggs. A mosquito's proboscis appears spike-solid, but it's actually a sheath of separate tools—cutting blades and a feeding tube powered by two tiny pumps. She drills through the epidermis, then through a thin layer of fat, then into the network of blood-filled micro-capillaries. She starts to drink.

To inhibit the blood from coagulating, the mosquito oils the bite area with a spray of saliva. This is when it happens. Carried in the mosquito's salivary glands—and entering the body with the lubricating squirt—are minute, wormlike creatures. These are the one-celled malaria parasites, known as plasmodia. Fifty thousand of them could swim in a pool the size of the period at the end of this sentence. Typically, a couple of dozen slip into the bloodstream. But it takes just one. A single plasmodium is enough to kill a person.

The parasites remain in the bloodstream for only a few minutes. They ride the flume of the circulatory system to the liver. There they stop. Each plasmodium burrows into a different liver cell. Almost certainly, the person who has been bitten hardly stirs from sleep. And for the next week or two, there's no overt sign that something in the body has just gone horribly wrong.

## Malaria Threatens Half the World's People

We live on a malarious planet. It may not seem that way from the vantage point of a wealthy country, where malaria is sometimes thought of, if it is thought of at all, as a problem that has mostly been solved, like smallpox or polio. In truth, malaria now affects more people than ever before. It's endemic to 106 nations, threatening half the world's population. In recent years, the parasite has grown so entrenched and has developed resistance to so many drugs that the most potent strains can scarcely be controlled. This year [2007] malaria will strike up to a half billion people. At least a million will die, most of them under age five, the vast majority living in Africa. That's more than twice the annual toll a generation ago.

The outcry over this epidemic, until recently, has been muted. Malaria is a plague of the poor, easy to overlook. The most unfortunate fact about malaria, some researchers believe, is that prosperous nations got rid of it. In the meantime, several distinctly unprosperous regions have reached the brink of total malarial collapse, virtually ruled by swarms of buzzing, flying syringes.

Only in the past few years has malaria captured the full attention of aid agencies and donors. The World Health Organization has made malaria reduction a chief priority. Bill Gates, who has called malaria "the worst thing on the planet," has donated hundreds of millions of dollars to the effort through the Bill and Melinda Gates Foundation. The [George W.] Bush Administration has pledged 1.2 billion dollars. Funds devoted to malaria have doubled since 2003. The idea is to disable the disease by combining virtually every known malaria-fighting technique, from the ancient (Chinese herbal medicines) to the old (bed nets) to the ultramodern (multidrug cocktails). At the same time, malaria researchers are pursuing a long-sought, elusive goal: a vaccine that would curb the disease for good. . . .

---

*Creating a malaria vaccine is one of the most ambitious medical quests of all time.*

---

Drugs, sprays, and nets, it appears, will never be more than part of the solution. What's required is an even more decisive weapon. "When I look at the whole malaria situation," says Louis Miller, co-chief of the malaria unit at the National Institute of Allergy and Infectious Diseases, "it all seems to come down to one basic idea: We sure need a vaccine."

## Malaria Vaccine Will Be Difficult to Develop

It's easy to list every vaccine that can prevent a parasitic disease in humans. There is none. Vaccines exist for bacteria and viruses, but these are comparatively simple organisms. The polio virus, for example, consists of exactly 11 genes. *Plasmodium falciparum* has more than 5,000. It's this complexity, combined with the malaria parasite's constant motion—dodging like a fugitive from the mosquito to the human bloodstream to the liver to the red blood cells—that makes a vaccine fiendishly difficult to design.

Ideally, a malaria vaccine would provide lifelong protection. A lull in malaria transmission could cause many people to lose any immunity they have built up against the disease—even adults, immunologically speaking, could revert to infant status—rendering it more devastating if it returned. This is why a partial victory over malaria could be worse than total failure. *Falciparum* also has countless substrains (each river valley seems to have its own type), and a vaccine has to block them all. And of course the vaccine can leave no opening for the parasite to develop resistance. Creating a malaria vaccine is one of the most ambitious medical quests of all time.

Recent malaria history is fraught with grand pronouncements that turned out to be baseless. "MALARIA VACCINE IS NEAR," announced a *New York Times* headline in 1984. "This is the last major hurdle," said one U.S. scientist quoted in the article. "There is no question now that we will have a vaccine. The rest is fine-tuning." Seven years of fine-tuning later, another *Times* headline summarized the result: "EFFORT TO FIGHT MALARIA APPEARS TO HAVE FAILED." In the late 1990s, Colombian immunologist Manuel Patarroyo claimed, with much media fanfare, that he had found the answer to malaria with his vaccine, SPf-66. Early results were tantalizing, but follow-up studies in Thailand showed it worked no better than a placebo.

## Ninety Research Teams at Work

At least 90 teams around the world are now working on some aspect of a vaccine; the British government, by way of incentive, has pledged to help purchase hundreds of millions of doses of any successful vaccine, for donation to countries in need. The one closest to public release, developed by the pharmaceutical company GlaxoSmithKline Biologicals in collaboration with the U.S. Army, is called RTS,S. In a recent trial in Mozambique, it protected about half the inoculated children from severe malaria for more than a year.

Fifty percent isn't bad—RTS,S might save hundreds of thousands of lives—but it's not the magic bullet that would neutralize the disease once and for all. Many researchers suspect an all-encompassing cure isn't possible. Malaria has always afflicted us, they say, and always will. There is one man, however, who not only believes malaria can be defeated, he thinks he knows the key.

Stephen Hoffman is the founder and CEO of the only company in the world dedicated solely to finding a malaria vaccine. The company's name is Sanaria—that is, "healthy air," the opposite of *malaria*. Hoffman is 58, lean and green-eyed, with a demeanor of single-minded intensity. "He's impassioned and impatient and intolerant of negativity," is how one colleague describes him.

Hoffman is intimately familiar with the pitfalls of the vaccine hunt. During his 14-year tenure as director of the malaria program at the Naval Medical Research Center, he was part of the team working on the vaccine promised in the 1984 *New York Times* article. He was so confident in the vaccine that he tested it on himself. He exposed himself to infected mosquitoes, then flew to a medical conference in California to deliver what he thought would be a triumphant presentation. The morning after he landed, he was already shaking and feverish—and, soon enough, suffering from full-blown malaria.

Now, more than two decades later, Hoffman is ready to return to prominence. He couldn't have found a more uninspiring launchpad: Sanaria is headquartered in a dismal mini-mall in suburban Maryland, near a picture-framing shop and a discount office-supply store. From outside, there's no mention of the company's mission. A window badly in need of washing bears the company name in tiny adhesive letters. Hoffman realizes it's probably best if the office-supply customers aren't fully aware of what's going on a few doors away.

## Raising Infected Mosquitos

Inside, generating a hubbub of activity, are some 30 scientists from across the globe. The lab's centerpiece is a room where Hoffman raises mosquitoes infected with the *falciparum* parasite—yes, in a quiet mini-mall. Hoffman claims it's the world's most secure insectary. To enter, a visitor must pass through multiple antechambers that are sealed between sets of doors, like a lock system in a canal. Everyone has to wear white cotton overlayers, masks, shoe covers, and gloves. White makes it easier to see a stray mosquito. The air is recirculated, and the insectary is checked daily for leaks. Signs abound: "WARN-ING! WARNING! INFECTIOUS AGENT IN USE." And hanging on a wall is a time-honored last line of defense: a flyswatter.

The mosquitoes are housed in a few dozen cylindrical containers, about the size of beach buckets, covered with mesh lids. They're fed *falciparum*-infected blood, then stored for two weeks while the parasites propagate in the insects' guts and migrate to the salivary glands, creating what are known as "loaded" mosquitoes. The loaded insects are transferred carefully to a kiln-like irradiator to be zapped with a quick dose of radiation. Then, in a special dissecting lab, the salivary glands of the mosquitoes are removed. Each mosquito's glands contain more than 100,000 parasites. Essentially, the vaccine consists of these irradiated parasites packed into a hypodermic needle.

---

*After so many million years on Earth and so many victories over humanity, [malaria], it is certain, will not surrender easily.*

---

The idea is based on research done in the late 1960s at New York University by Ruth Nussenzweig, who demonstrated that parasites weakened by radiation can prompt an immune response in mice without causing malaria. Hoffman's vaccine will deliver the wallop of a thousand mosquito bites and, he says, produce a complete protective response. Thereafter, any time the vaccinated person is bitten by a malaria-carrying mosquito, the body, already in a state of alert, will not allow the disease to take hold.

Hoffman's lofty goal is to eventually immunize all 25 million infants born in sub-Saharan Africa every year. He believes that at least 90 percent of them will be protected completely from malaria. If so, they'll be the first generation of Africans, in all of human history, not to suffer from the disease.

But which generation will it be? Although Sanaria's vaccine may undergo initial field-testing [in 2009], a federally approved version won't be available for at least five years—and maybe never. Given the track record of malaria vaccines, that's a distinct possibility. After so many million years on Earth and so many victories over humanity, the disease, it is certain, will not surrender easily.

When it comes to malaria, only one thing is guaranteed: Every evening in the rainy season across much of the world, *Anopheles* mosquitoes will take wing, alert to the odors and warmth of living bodies. A female *Anopheles* needs to drink blood every three days. In a single feeding, which lasts as long as ten minutes, she can ingest about two and a half times her pre-meal weight—in human terms, the equivalent of downing a bathtub-size milk shake.

If she happens to feed on a person infected with malaria, parasites will accompany the blood. Two weeks later, when the mosquito flies through the open window of a mud hut, seeking her next meal, she'll be loaded.

Inside the hut, a child is sleeping with her sister and parents on a blanket spread over the floor. The family is aware of the malaria threat; they know of the rainy season's dangers. They've hung a bed net from the ceiling. But it's a steamy night, and the child has tossed and turned a few times before dropping back to sleep. Her foot is sticking out of the net. The mosquito senses it, and dips down for a silent landing.

# Vaccines Are Being Developed to Treat Cancer

*Michelle Meadows*

*Michelle Meadows is a staff writer for* FDA Consumer, *a bimonthly publication of the U.S. Food and Drug Administration.*

Vaccines traditionally have been used to prevent infectious diseases such as measles and the flu. But with cancer vaccines, the emphasis is on treatment, at least for now. The idea is to inject a preparation of inactivated cancer cells or proteins that are unique to cancer cells into a person who has cancer. The goal: to train the person's immune system to recognize the living cancer cells and attack them.

"The best settings are for treating people who have minimal disease or a high risk of recurrence," says Jeffrey Schlom, Ph.D., chief of the Laboratory of Tumor Immunology and Biology at the National Cancer Institute (NCI). "But at this time, most therapeutic cancer vaccines are being studied in people who have failed other therapies."

Cancer vaccines are experimental; none have been licensed by the Food and Drug Administration [FDA]. But there are about a dozen cancer vaccines in advanced clinical trials, says Steven Hirschfeld, M.D., a medical officer in the FDA's Center for Biologics Evaluation and Research. "Research has shown us that the fundamental approach to cancer vaccines is right; we are moving in the right direction," he says.

The three standard cancer therapies are surgery to remove tumors; chemotherapy, which modifies or destroys cancer cells with drugs; and radiation, which destroys cancer cells with high-energy X-rays. Immunotherapy, which includes cancer vaccines, is considered a fourth, and still investigational, type

Michelle Meadows, "Cancer Vaccines: Training the Immune System to Fight Cancer," *FDA Consumer Magazine*, September/October 2004.

of therapy. Cancer vaccines are sometimes used alone, but are often combined with a standard therapy.

While standard treatments alone have proven effective, they also have limitations. Radiation and chemotherapy can wipe out a person's cancer cells, but they also damage normal cells. "We want to find treatment that is more targeted and less toxic," says Hirschfeld. "Cancer vaccines are designed to be specific, targeting only the cancer cells without harming the healthy ones."

The approach has made cancer vaccines generally well tolerated, allowing them to be used in outpatient settings. And they can be added to standard therapy with a low likelihood of causing further serious side effects.

## How Cancer Vaccines Work

Cancer is a term for more than 100 diseases characterized by the uncontrolled, abnormal growth of cells. To the immune system—the body's natural defense system against disease—cancer cells and normal cells look the same. The immune system tends to tolerate the cancer cells, just as it tolerates the normal cells. That's because the immune system doesn't recognize cancer cells as something foreign, Hirschfeld says. Rather, cancer cells are once-normal cells that have gone awry. Cancer vaccines try to get the immune system to overcome its tolerance of cancer cells so that it can recognize them and attack them.

All cells have unique proteins or bits of proteins on their surface called antigens. Many cancer cells make cancer-specific antigens. The goal of using cancer antigens as a vaccine is to teach the immune system to recognize the cancer-specific antigens and to reject any cells with those antigens. The antigens activate white blood cells called B lymphocytes (B cells) and T lymphocytes (T cells). B cells produce antibodies that recognize a particular antigen and bind to it to help destroy the cancer cells. T cells that recognize a particular antigen can attack and kill cancer cells. In 1991, the first human cancer antigen was found in cells of a person with melanoma, a discovery that encouraged researchers to search for antigens on other types of cancer, according to the NCI.

---

*Researchers have been working to develop cancer vaccines for more than 100 years in one form or another.*

---

The two main approaches for cancer vaccines are whole-cell vaccines and antigen vaccines. Whole-cell vaccines may take whole cancer cells from a patient or sometimes several patients, or use human tumor cell lines derived in a laboratory. "Some cell-based vaccines use tumor cells from the patient, some contain something that looks like a tumor cell but was created in a lab, and others are personalized vaccines that use some cells from the patient and some from the lab," Hirschfeld says. Cells that are taken from people with cancer are altered in a lab to inactivate them so that they are safe to re-inject.

Regardless of the exact source of the cells, whole cell vaccines potentially use all the antigens found on the tumor cells. Antigen vaccines try to trigger an immune response by using only certain antigens from cancer cells. Hirschfeld says antigens may be particular to an individual, to a certain type of cancer, or to several types of cancers.

## Boosting the Immune Response

In the early 1990s, Steven Rosenberg, M.D., one of the pioneers of immunotherapy and chief of surgery at the NCI, wrote that trying to use the immune system to fight cancer is so difficult that it made him feel "like a dog trying to bite a basketball." Among Rosenberg's contributions was identifying the antigens that trigger an immune response, and cloning genes that look for, or "code for," those antigens.

Researchers have been working to develop cancer vaccines for more than 100 years in one form or another, and the main mission has always been to make the immune system's response to the cancer antigens as strong as possible.

One major strategy involves combining vaccines with additional substances called adjuvants, which act as chemical messengers that help T cells work better. An example of one type of adjuvant, called a cytokine, is interleukin-2. This protein is made by the body's immune system and can also be made in a lab.

There have also been improvements in vaccine delivery. For example, Schlom developed a vaccine in which genes for tumor antigens are put into a weakened virus called a "vector" that delivers genetic materials to cells. This makes the tumor antigen more visible to the immune system. The CEA-TRICOM vaccine was developed at the NCI through a cooperative research and development agreement with Therion Biologics in Cambridge, Mass. Researchers use the *vaccinia* virus, the same virus in the smallpox vaccine, as the vector. The carcinoembryonic antigen (CEA), which is found on most breast, lung, colon, and pancreatic tumors, is added to the virus. Researchers also add three molecules, called "costimulatory molecules," which serve as signals that make the vaccine more potent than it would be if the antigen were used alone. A similar vaccine developed under the NCI agreement with Therion is the PANVAC vaccine, which has now entered advanced study as a treatment for pancreatic cancer.

In addition to studying this type of virus-based technique, researchers at Duke University's Cancer Center in Durham, N.C., have been studying vaccines that mix white blood cells called dendritic cells with genetic material from a person's tumor.

Dendritic cells, which can activate T cells, work by looking around, finding antigens, and showing them to the fighter T cells. Researchers have found ways to increase the number of dendritic cells in a vaccine. "Employing millions of 'pumped up' dendritic cells can help elicit a strong immune response," says H. Kim Lyerly, M.D., director of the Duke cancer center.

---

*Cancer vaccines have shown promise in clinical trials with many types of cancer.*

---

Recent work by Lyerly and Duke investigators Michael Morse, M.D., and Timothy Clay, Ph.D., has focused on modifying dendritic cells with viruses so that they activate even stronger T cell responses against cancer antigens.

"This is an evolving area, and it's exciting to be able to make progress," says Lyerly. "For decades, people thought it wasn't even fundamentally possible to develop cancer vaccines, and here we are. The science behind cancer vaccines is leading us to believe that we will find the answers."

## Promising, but Still Early

As with any new treatment, cancer vaccines must be first studied in lab animals and then tested for safety and effectiveness in three phases of human studies, called "clinical trials," before they can be approved by the FDA. In Phase 1 clinical trials, cancer vaccines are used alone and studied for safety and to determine the proper dose. In Phase 2 trials, they are tested for effectiveness and may be used alone or in combination with another therapy. Phase 3 trials are large-scale studies testing effectiveness and usually comparing a vaccine with some standard therapy. Researchers are testing vaccines using various adjuvants, delivery methods, and types of antigens.

Cancer vaccines have shown promise in clinical trials with many types of cancer. According to Howard Streicher, M.D., a senior investigator with the NCI's Cancer Therapy Evaluation Program, it's too soon to say which cancers will be treated with vaccine therapy. The types of tumors that have proven most susceptible to vaccines so far, he says, are: skin cancer (melanoma); kidney cancer (renal cell); a group of cancers that affect the lymphatic system (lymphoma); a malignant tumor of the bone marrow (myeloma); and solid tumors, such as lung cancer. The most work has been done in the area of melanoma, a type of skin cancer in which treatment options are limited when the disease is in advanced stages.

"After having a tumor removed, about half of patients with stage III melanoma may have a recurrence, and we want to prevent that," Streicher says. "Chemotherapy doesn't work in this area, so our hope is that this could be just the right place for a vaccine."

James Mulé, M.D., Ph.D., associate director of the H. Lee Moffitt Cancer Center and Research Institute in Tampa, Fla., says, though some early studies have shown that some people's tumors shrank or even disappeared in response to a cancer vaccine, it's still early. Mulé was an investigator on the first study that tested dendritic cells in children. In the Phase 1 study, one 16-year-old with cancer that had spread to her lungs and spine showed significant shrinkage of tumors.

"There is promise in the sense that some of these vaccines can illicit a powerful immune response in some patients, but I think we have to be careful about getting too excited over early studies that can't be reproduced," Mulé says. . . .

## No Cancer Vaccine Licensed Yet

Experts say that no therapeutic cancer vaccine has been licensed yet because few Phase 3 studies have been completed, and those that have been completed did not meet their goals of demonstrating safety and effectiveness of the vaccine. "We are still working with industry to define the characteristics, including potency," says the FDA's Hirschfeld. "So a trial may look promising early on, but our job is to make sure it can be reproduced. We have to ask: 'Will this treatment work in the larger population?'"

One of the challenges is that cancer vaccines may produce different effects than those caused by cancer drugs. With cancer drugs, experts ask whether there is an objective, measurable response, such as tumor shrinkage. A cancer drug may cause tumors to shrink, but a person still may not live longer. With a cancer vaccine, there may be fewer signs of tumor shrinkage, but a person might live longer. . . .

Cancer researchers say their work won't mean much if more people don't enroll in clinical trials. According to the NCI, less than 3 percent of U.S. adults with cancer participate in clinical trials.

If there is a standard treatment available for a type of cancer, the NCI recommends choosing it over an experimental therapy. Cancer vaccines show the most promise at preventing a recurrence of cancer after surgery, radiation, or chemotherapy because the immune system will need to recognize and attack a smaller number of cancer cells. Cancer vaccines are also being tested as a treatment for advanced cancer.

---

*Though most cancer vaccines have been well-tolerated, . . . some people have experienced autoimmune problems.*

---

Gary Montgomery, 66, of Redmond, Wash., enrolled in a cancer vaccine trial in 2002 to treat a rare form of abdominal cancer called pseudomyxoma peritonei. According to the National Organization for Rare Disorders, the disease is characterized by the accumulation of mucus-secreting tumor cells in the abdomen and pelvis. As the mass of tumor cells grows, the abdomen swells and digestive function becomes impaired.

Montgomery first had the standard therapy of surgery to remove the tumors in 2000. "They opened me up like a sardine can—from the sternum to the abdomen—and took out as many tumors as possible," Montgomery says. Then they inserted a tube into the abdomen, which delivered chemotherapy for six months. He experienced no tumor growth for about a year, but then the tumors came back. "It's known as a relentless form of cancer that wears you down," he says. "The doctor said that with the exception of another surgery, there was really nothing else they could do."

So Montgomery started with the Internet and found one NCI study that involved surgery and chemotherapy with an agent different from the one he had before. But the trial was closed. Taking advice from a friend, he checked at the Lombardi Cancer Center at Georgetown University in Washington, D.C. "I was feeling pretty low at this point," he says. He found out the one vaccine study he was interested in had just ended. But a nurse told him that another trial with newer versions of cancer vaccines developed at the NCI was about to start. "There were two slots left," he says. "Luckily, I met the criteria."

Montgomery received a "prime-boost regimen" of Therion Biologics' TRICOM vaccine. He first received an injection in the upper leg of a modified version of the smallpox vaccine to prime the immune system. Then he received monthly boosters of a vaccine called fowlpox CEA (carcinoembryonic antigen), an antigen found on most colorectal and pancreatic cancers. He also received a shot of the hormone GM-CSF, which helps stimulate the cells of the immune system. He had to give some of the injections to himself when he arrived back home in Washington state.

He says he experienced minimal side effects, such as soreness at the site of injection and mild flu-like symptoms. Though most cancer vaccines have been well-tolerated, in other trials some people have experienced autoimmune problems such as inflammation of the thyroid gland, skin disorders, and colitis. Autoimmune conditions are those in which the immune system mistakenly attacks the body's tissues and organs. Before he began the trial, Montgomery signed an informed consent form acknowledging that he was aware of all the risks.

Montgomery continues to participate in the trial and flies to the nation's capital every month to receive treatment because it's been working. "It hasn't cured the cancer," Montgomery says, "but it seems to be keeping it in check. And that's good enough for me."

# New Vaccines May Help Stop Smoking, Drug Use, and Overeating

*Ronald Kotulak*

*Ronald Kotulak is a Pulitzer Prize–winning journalist who writes about science for the* Chicago Tribune.

Vaccines, the most potent medical weapon ever devised to vanquish deadly germs, are now being called on to do something totally different and culturally revolutionary—inoculate people against bad habits like overeating, cigarette smoking and drug use.

Whether this new era of vaccine research can actually subdue many of the poor lifestyle choices that are today's biggest threats to health—causing obesity, cancer, heart disease and other problems—has yet to be proved.

But the evidence is promising enough to persuade the federal government to put millions of dollars toward finding out if two of the vaccines can end nicotine and cocaine addiction.

The National Institute on Drug Abuse, which has spent $15 million on clinical trials for the vaccines and plans to spend more, predicts that one of the nicotine vaccines may be available for marketing [by the end of 2009].

"The American Cancer Society has projected that we will have 1 billion people die from smoking in the world in this century," said Frank Vocci, director of medications development for the institute. "If you had a vaccine that helped people quit and stay quit, or prevent them from smoking, that's where you'd get the greatest public health benefit."

Meanwhile, results from a major obesity vaccine trial under way in Switzerland are expected [in late 2006] and company officials are hopeful that the vaccine could be ready for use in a few years.

## New Vaccine Technology

To stamp out deleterious behavior, the new vaccines employ the body's natural immune system in an innovative way. Instead of building antibodies to destroy germs as traditional vaccines do, they construct antibodies that lock onto nicotine and cocaine molecules, preventing them from reaching the brain.

"What we're seeing is a renaissance in vaccine technology," said Dr. Gary Nabel, director of the National Institute of Allergy and Infectious Diseases' Vaccine Research Center. "It's only natural that when you have a technology that's this powerful it can be applied to other medical problems."

Normally, nicotine and cocaine molecules are too small to be seen by the immune system. So to make the vaccines, scientists attach these molecules to big target proteins, such as harmless viruses or bacteria, which the immune system can recognize and attack with specialized antibodies.

When the person later smokes a cigarette or takes cocaine, the antibodies wrap up and neutralize the molecules before they can trigger feelings of euphoria and pleasure in the brain. Smokers and cocaine users given the vaccines say their pleasure is diminished or they no longer get as high, which decreases the desire for the drug.

"I'm trying to cut back because cigarettes don't taste so good anymore," said James VanHall, a truck driver for the City of Minneapolis who is participating in a trial of the anti-nicotine vaccine at the University of Minnesota. Although he doesn't know if the three shots he has received [so far] are the vaccine or a placebo, VanHall says he can tell they are having an effect.

"Cigarettes pretty much tasted good all my life, but right now it seems like I'm smoking a light cigarette or something," said VanHall, 50, who has been smoking since his early teens and would go through a pack or a pack and a half a day. "There's hardly any flavor there. I'm hoping the vaccine works because this is the worst thing I've ever tried to quit in my life."

Several months into the study, VanHall stopped smoking altogether. It's hard, he said, but he has less craving for cigarettes now than when he tried to quit in the past.

In the case of the obesity vaccine, antibodies attach to the hunger protein called ghrelin, preventing it from reaching the brain and stimulating appetite.

Ghrelin, which is secreted by the empty stomach, travels in the bloodstream to the brain, where it tells a person to eat. But the hormone, discovered in 1999, also has other important roles, such as signaling the body to become less active and to store food as fat instead of using it for energy production.

---

*To many researchers the vaccines seem to be a potential answer to many of society's major ills.*

---

The reason it can be so hard to lose weight, researchers believe, is that dieting causes large amounts of ghrelin to be produced as the body seeks to stimulate eating, slow down the metabolism of fat and promote fat retention. Ghrelin also may help explain the yo-yo experience of millions of people who try to lose weight but end up putting on more pounds.

"What happens after many attempts at dieting is that you lose weight but as soon as you stop dieting and go back on normal feeding your ghrelin levels rise again and that makes you have a lot of hunger," said immunologist Claudine Blaser of the Swiss company Cytos, whose obesity vaccine is undergoing clinical trials in 100 people.

In experiments with mice, the animals given the vaccine reduced their weight gain by 15 percent to 20 percent even though they ate as much as other mice that became obese. Researchers also found they burned off more fat, making them leaner.

## Helping Smokers to Quit

Cytos also is in advanced stages of testing a nicotine vaccine. Earlier studies showed that 42 percent of smokers receiving the vaccine remained abstinent after a year, compared with 21 percent who got a placebo shot.

"What we can do with our vaccine approach is to basically help these people get off their bad habits and get off their risks of developing severe chronic diseases later on," Blaser said.

The U.S. Food and Drug Administration recently put another nicotine vaccine, NicVAX, on a fast-track status so it can be rushed to market if shown to be safe and effective. Nabi Biopharmaceuticals, a biotech company in Boca Raton, Fla., is expanding trials of NicVAX after a study showed 40 percent of the people getting the vaccine were smoke-free after six months, compared with 9 percent receiving a placebo.

To many researchers the vaccines seem to be a potential answer to many of society's major ills—in the U.S. there are 50 million cigarette smokers, 5 million drug addicts, 60 million obese adults and 9 million overweight youngsters between ages 6 and 19.

Most have one thing in common: They'd like to quit but can't. Nearly 7 out of 10 smokers, for instance, say they want to stop, but 80 percent to 90 percent of those who try to quit resume smoking within a year. The relapse problem is even worse for cocaine addicts.

"There is a great deal of promise for the nicotine vaccine not only as a smoking cessation tool but also potentially as a relapse prevention tool," said Dorothy Hatsukami, director of the Transdisciplinary Tobacco Use Research Center at the University of Minnesota Cancer Center.

---

*Unlike most older vaccines, which tend to confer permanent immunity, the new breed of vaccines is reversible.*

---

"For those who have achieved abstinence and don't want to slip into relapse, being injected by the vaccine might be a good tool," said Hatsukami, whose preliminary data showed that in a small group of smokers the nicotine vaccine enabled 38 percent to remain abstinent for 30 days compared with 9 percent on a placebo.

The goal is getting people to give up cigarettes for a year. "If you can get someone past 12 months with being smoke-free, there's a 70 to 75 percent chance that that person will remain smoke-free," said Nabi official Thomas Rathjen.

Unlike most older vaccines, which tend to confer permanent immunity, the new breed of vaccines is reversible, providing immunity against nicotine, cocaine or the hunger hormone ghrelin for one to three months before booster shots are needed. None of the new vaccines has produced side effects other than some flulike symptoms and soreness at the injection site.

"These vaccines are not going to be a panacea for treating everything," said Kim Janda of the Scripps Research Institute, a pioneer in developing vaccines for addiction and obesity. "I believe they can be helpful. When people are undergoing abstinence for drugs of abuse and they have weak moments, if you have a vaccine in place it can assist them so they don't spiral down to ground zero."

# Organizations to Contact

*The editors have compiled the following list of organizations concerned with the issues debated in this book. The descriptions are derived from materials provided by the organizations. All have publications or information available for interested readers. The list was compiled on the date of publication of the present volume; the information provided here may change. Be aware that many organizations take several weeks or longer to respond to inquiries, so allow as much time as possible.*

### Advocates for Children's Health Affected by Mercury Poisoning (A-CHAMP)
e-mail: info@a-champ.org
Web site: www.a-champ.org

A-CHAMP is a national, nonpartisan political action organization formed by parents in support of children with neurodevelopmental and communication disorders. It is dedicated to advancing public policy issues affecting children, protecting their human and civil rights, educating the public and media, and supporting candidates sharing its goals in state and federal elections. Its Web site contains many links to information resources, including government documents.

### Anthrax Vaccine Immunization Program (AVIP)
(877) 438-8222 • fax: (703) 681-4692
e-mail: vaccines@amedd.army.mil
Web site: www.anthrax.osd.mil

AVIP is the U.S. military anthrax immunization program. Its official Web site contains detailed information about the use of anthrax as a biological weapon, the disease itself, and the effects of the vaccine. Its aim is to convince readers that the threat of an anthrax attack against the military is real and that the vaccine is safe.

**Center for Bioethics**
3401 Market St., Suite 320, Philadelphia, PA   19104
(215) 898-7136
Web site: www.bioethics.upenn.edu

A research organization affiliated with the University of Pennsylvania, the Center for Bioethics has identified and studied ethical challenges present throughout the vaccine life cycle; organized regional, national, and international meetings; and contributed to the scholarly and public dialogues on vaccine ethics and policy.

**Center for Biologics Evaluation and Research (CBER)**
Food and Drug Administration, Rockville, MD   20852-1448
(800) 835-4709
e-mail: octma@cber.fda.gov
Web site: www.fda.gov/cber/vaccines.htm

The Center for Biologics Evaluation and Research (CBER), part of the Food and Drug Administration (FDA), is the U.S. government agency that regulates vaccine products. Its Web site contains extensive information about vaccines, the FDA approval process, and preparation for epidemics or bioterrorist attacks.

**Centers for Disease Control and Prevention (CDC)**
1600 Clifton Rd., Atlanta, GA   30333
(800) 232-4636 • fax: (770) 488-4760
Web site: www.cdc.gov/vaccines

The CDC is the public health agency of the U.S. Department of Health and Human Services. The agency promotes health and quality of life by preventing and controlling disease, injury, and disability. Its Web site offers extensive information about infectious diseases and vaccines, as well as many links to government resources.

## Childhood Influenza Immunization Coalition (CIIC)
90 Fifth Ave., Suite 800, New York, NY   10011-2052
(212) 886-2277
e-mail: CIIC@nfid.org
Web site: www.preventchildhoodinfluenza.org

The CIIC was established by the National Foundation for Infectious Diseases (NFID) to protect infants, children, and adolescents from influenza by communicating the need to make influenza immunization a national health priority and by seeking to improve the low influenza immunization rates among children. The CIIC Web site offers information sheets and links to its member organizations.

## Children's Hospital of Philadelphia Vaccine Education Center
The Children's Hospital of Philadelphia
Philadelphia, Pa   19104
(215) 590-9990
Web site: www.vaccine.chop.edu

The Children's Hospital of Philadelphia is committed to exceptional patient care, training new generations of pediatric health care providers, and pioneering significant research initiatives. Its Vaccine Education Center Web site contains detailed information about each available vaccine, plus answers to general questions about vaccination.

## Coalition for SafeMinds
254 Trickum Creek Rd., Tyrone, GA   30290
(404) 934-0777
e-mail: eksafeminds@gmail.com
Web site: www.safeminds.org

The Coalition for SafeMinds (Sensible Action For Ending Mercury-Induced Neurological Disorders) is a private non-profit organization founded to investigate and raise awareness of the risks to infants and children of exposure to mercury from medical products, including thimerosal in vaccines. It focuses on the growing evidence of a link between mercury and neurological disorders, such as autism, attention deficit disorder, language delay, and learning difficulties. Its Web site contains informational brochures on vaccine research and government policy that can be downloaded.

### Every Child By Two (ECBT)
666 Eleventh St. NW, Suite 202Z
Washington, DC   20001-4542
(202) 783-7034 • fax: (202) 783-7042
Web site: www.ecbt.org

Every Child By Two works in conjunction with the Centers for Disease Control and Prevention (CDC) to conduct educational programs for health care providers. Its aim is to educate those who effect policy decisions regarding immunizations and to seek funding for state immunization programs. Its Web site offers a variety of resources and contacts.

### Immunization Action Coalition (IAC)
1573 Selby Ave., Suite 234, St. Paul, MN   55104
(651) 647-9009 • fax: (651) 647-9131
e-mail: admin@immunize.org
Web site: www.immunize.org

The Immunization Action Coalition works to increase immunization rates and prevent disease by creating and distributing educational materials for health professionals and the public that enhance the delivery of safe and effective immunization services. It facilitates communication about the safety, efficacy, and use of vaccines within the broad immunization community of patients, parents, health care organizations, and government health agencies. IAC publishes three periodicals: *Needle Tips*, *Vaccinate Adults*, and *Vaccinate Women*.

**Infectious Diseases Society of America (IDSA)**
1300 Wilson Blvd., Suite 300, Arlington, VA   22209
(703) 299-0200 • fax: (703) 299-0204
Web site: www.idsociety.org

IDSA represents physicians, Scientists, and other health care professionals who specialize in infectious diseases. Its Web site is designed mainly for these professionals but contains information of interest to the public about specific diseases and the need for immunization.

**Institute for Vaccine Safety**
Johns Hopkins University Bloomberg School of Public Health
Baltimore, MD   21205
Web site: www.vaccinesafety.edu

The Institute for Vaccine Safety is operated by the Johns Hopkins University Bloomberg School of Public Health. Its mission is to provide an independent assessment of vaccines and vaccine safety to help guide decision makers and educate physicians, the public, and the media about key issues surrounding the safety of vaccines and to work toward preventing disease using the safest vaccines possible. Its Web site contains many annotated links to information about specific diseases and vaccines.

**Military & Biodefense Vaccine Project (MBVP)**
National Vaccine Information Center, Vienna, VA   22180
e-mail: contact@military-biodefensevaccines.org
Web site: www.military-biodefensevaccines.org

The Military & Biodefense Vaccine Project is sponsored by the National Vaccine Information Center. It focuses on the safety and effectiveness of vaccines that are being developed for routine use in the military or for use by military personnel and civilians in response to bioterror threats. Its Web site provides information resources and links to relevant news articles.

**Military Vaccine Agency (MILVAX)**
(877) 438-8222 • fax: (703) 681-4692
e-mail: vaccines@amedd.army.mil
Web site: www.vaccines.mil

MILVAX works to enhance military medical readiness and protect human health by synchronizing information, delivering education, enhancing scientific understanding, promoting quality, and coordinating military immunization programs worldwide. It supports all five branches of the armed services. Its Web site contains detailed information about diseases, vaccines, and policies.

**National Foundation for Infectious Diseases (NFID)**
4733 Bethesda Ave., Suite 750, Bethesda, Maryland 20814
(301) 656-0003 • fax: (301) 907-0878
e-mail: info@nfid.org
Web site: www.nfid.org

The National Foundation for Infectious Diseases (NFID) is a nonprofit organization dedicated to educating the public and health care professionals about the causes, treatment, and prevention of infectious diseases. It publishes factsheets and promotional material focused mainly on immunization of adolescents and adults.

**National Network for Immunization Information (NNII)**
301 University Blvd. CH 2.218, Galveston, TX 77555-0351
(409) 772-0199 • fax: (409) 747-4995
e-mail: nnii@i4ph.org
Web site: www.immunizationinfo.org

The aim of the NNII is to provide the public, health professionals, policy makers, and the media with up-to-date, scientifically valid information related to immunization in order to help all stakeholders understand the issues and make informed decisions. Its Web site has information about many specific diseases and the vaccines available to prevent them.

**National Vaccine Information Center (NVIC)**
204 Mill St., Suite B1, Vienna, VA   22180
(703) 938-0342 • fax: (703) 938-5768
Web site: www.nvic.org

The National Vaccine Information Center, a national non-profit educational organization, advocates for vaccine safety and informed-consent protections in the current mandatory vaccination system. It is dedicated to the prevention of vaccine injuries and deaths through public education. As an independent clearinghouse for information on diseases and vaccines, NVIC does not promote either the use or refusal of vaccines; instead, it supports the availability of all preventive health care options and the right of consumers to make educated, voluntary health care choices.

**PATH Vaccine Resource Library**
1455 NW Leary Way, Seattle, WA   98107
(206) 285-3500 • fax: (206) 285-6619
e-mail: info@path.org
Web site: www.path.org/vaccineresources

PATH is an international nonprofit organization that creates sustainable, culturally relevant solutions enabling communities worldwide to break longstanding cycles of poor health. Its Vaccine Resources Library offers a wide variety of scientifically based documents on vaccine-preventable diseases and topics in immunization. In addition to resources developed at PATH, the library contains materials published by the U.S. Centers for Disease Control and Prevention, the World Health Organization, the Global Alliance for Vaccines and Immunization, and many others.

**Protecting Our Guardians (POG)**
e-mail: protecting.our.guardians@charter.net
Web site: www.protectingourguardians.org

POG is a nonprofit organization dedicated to protecting military members from the anthrax vaccine and the Anthrax Vaccine Immunization Program (AVIP), which it views as hazardous, and to supporting safe alternatives. It is a military family advocacy group composed of doctors, nurses, veterans, military families, and concerned citizens. Its Web site includes links to pages about the side effects of the vaccine, the bioterrorist threat, information about manufacturers, current litigation, and related Web sites.

**Vaccination News**
PO Box 111818, Anchorage, AK   99511-1818
e-mail: sandy@vaccinationnews.com
Web site: http:/vaccinationnews.com

Vaccination News is a nonprofit corporation that presents a wide range of current news and views on vaccinations and vaccination policy, covering all sides of the vaccination controversy. Its Web Site is updated daily.

# Bibliography

## Books

Arthur Allen — *Vaccine: The Controversial Story of Medicine's Greatest Lifesaver.* New York: Norton, 2007.

Robert Baker — *Quiet Killers: The Fall and Rise of Deadly Diseases.* Stroud, UK: Sutton, 2008.

Debbie Bookchin and Jim Schumacher — *The Virus and the Vaccine: The True Story of a Cancer-Causing Monkey Virus, Contaminated Polio Vaccine, and the Millions of Americans Exposed.* New York: St. Martin's, 2004.

Tammy Boyce — *Health Risk and News: The MMR Vaccine and the Media.* New York: Peter Lang, 2007.

John Clifton — *Stop the Shots! Are Vaccinations Killing Our Pets?* New York: Foley Square, 2007.

James Colgrove — *State of Immunity: The Politics of Vaccination in Twentieth-Century America.* Berkeley and Los Angeles: University of California Press, 2007.

Michael Fitzpatrick — *MMR and Autism: What Parents Need to Know.* New York: Routledge, 2004.

Jacob Heller — *The Vaccine Narrative.* Nashville: Vanderbilt University Press, 2008.

Richard Horton     *A Jab in the Dark: Anxiety and Rationality in the MMR Vaccine Controversy.* New York: New York Review of Books, 2005.

Ann Janetta     *The Vaccinators: Smallpox, Medical Knowledge, and the "Opening" of Japan.* Stanford, CA: Stanford University Press, 2007.

Patricia Kahn, ed.     *AIDS Vaccine Handbook.* New York: AIDS Vaccine Advocacy Coalition, 2005.

David Kirby     *Evidence of Harm: Mercury in Vaccines and the Autism Epidemic—a Medical Controversy.* New York: St. Martin's, 2005.

Melissa Leach and     *Vaccine Anxieties: Global Science,*
James Fairhead     *Child Health and Society.* Sterling, VA: Earthscan, 2007.

Kurt Link     *The Vaccine Controversy: The History, Use, and Safety of Vaccinations.* Westport, CT: Praeger, 2005.

Gary Matsumoto     *Vaccine A: The Covert Government Experiment That's Killing Our Soldiers—and Why GI's Are Only the First Victims.* New York: Basic Books, 2004.

Neil Z. Miller     *Vaccine Safety Manual for Concerned Families and Health Practitioners: Guide to Immunization Risks and Protection.* Santa Fe, NM: New Atlantean, 2008.

| Neil Z. Miller and Bernard Rimland | *Vaccines, Autism and Childhood Disorders: Crucial Data That Could Save Your Child's Life.* Santa Fe, NM: New Atlantean, 2008 |
|---|---|
| Catherine M. O'Driscoll | *What Vets Don't Tell You About Vaccines.* Derbyshire, UK: Abbeywood, 2007. |
| Paul A. Offit | *The Cutter Incident: How America's First Polio Vaccine Led to the Growing Vaccine Crisis.* New Haven, CT: Yale University Press, 2007. |
| Paul A. Offit | *Vaccinated: One Man's Quest to Defeat the World's Deadliest Diseases.* New York: HarperCollins, 2007. |
| Paul A. Offit and Louis M. Bell | *Vaccines: What You Should Know.* Hoboken, NJ: Wiley, 2003. |
| Mark Orrin and Gary S. Goldman, eds. | *The Chickenpox Vaccine: A New Epidemic of Disease and Corruption.* Pearblossom, CA: Medical Veritas International, 2006. |
| Ciro A. de Quadros, ed. | *Vaccines: Preventing Disease and Protecting Health.* Washington, DC: Pan American Health Organization, 2004. |
| David Rosner and Gerald Markowitz | *Are We Ready? Public Health Since 9/11.* Berkeley and Los Angeles: University of California Press, 2006. |
| Robert Sears | *The Vaccine Book.* New York: Little, Brown, 2007. |

Sherri J.
Tenpenny
*Vaccines: The Risks, the Benefits, the Choices: A Resource Guide for Parents.* Sevierville, TN: Insight, 2006.

## Periodicals

Mary Carmichael et al.
"A Shot of Hope," *Newsweek*, October 1, 2007.

Jim Giles
"Why Vaccines Are Hard to Swallow," *New Scientist*, January 26, 2008.

Serena Gordon
"Kids' Vaccine Ingredient Not Likely Linked to Neurological Problems," *U.S. News and World Report*, September 26, 2007.

Hilary Hilton
"A Drug to End Drug Addiction," *Time*, January 8, 2008.

Jeneen Interlandi
"The Anti-Drug Drugs," *Newsweek*, January 3, 2008.

Richard G. Judelsohn
"Vaccine Safety: Vaccines Are One of Public Health's Great Accomplishments," *Skeptical Inquirer*, November 8, 2007.

Sean Kennedy
"Eulogy for a Doomed Vaccine," *Advocate*, January 29, 2008.

Charles Krauthammer
"Smallpox Shots: Make Them Mandatory," *Time*, December 15, 2002.

Robert Langreth
"Booster Shot," *Forbes*, November 12, 2007.

| Diana Lynne | "Newborn Vaccinated over Parents' Objections," *Whistleblower*, April 2007. |
| Brendan Maher | "Malaria: The End of the Beginning," *Nature*, February 28, 2008. |
| Donald G. McNeil Jr. | "The Soul of a New Vaccine," *New York Times*, December 11, 2007. |
| Lindsey O'Connor | "The HPV Vaccine," *Today's Christian Woman*, July/August 2007. |
| Alice Park | "Assessing a Failed AIDS Vaccine," *Time*, November 7, 2007. |
| Steven Reinberg | "Vaccines for Ovarian and Breast Cancer in Early Trials," *HealthDay*, January 12, 2008. |
| Jessica Snyder Sachs | "Rebooting the AIDS Vaccine," *Popular Science*, January 2008. |
| Suzanne Sataline | "No Vaccine Link to Behavior," *Wall Street Journal*, September 26, 2007. |
| Julia Scirrotto | "Sex, Lies and the HPV Vaccine," *Marie Claire*, February 2008. |
| Sherrill Sellman | "Beware of Wolves in Sheep's Clothing," *Total Health*, March/April 2007. |
| Nancy Shute | "New Studies Reveal a Genetic Cause and Find No Connection to Shots Containing Thimerosal," *U.S. News and World Report*, January 7, 2008. |

Nancy Schute      "On Parenting: Genes—Not Vaccines—Linked to Autism," *U.S. News and World Report*, January 9, 2008

Nancy Shute      "On Parenting: Reassuring Autism Findings," *U.S. News and World Report*, January 7, 2008.

Barbara Simpson      "Medical Terrorists at Your Doorstep," *Whistleblower*, 2007.

Alexandra M. Stewart      "Mandating HPV Vaccination—Private Rights, Public Good," *New England Journal of Medicine*, May 10, 2007.

Sherri Tenpenny      "Vaccinations and the Right to Refuse," *Whistleblower*, April 2007.

Bob Unruh      "Civilians Could Face Mandatory Anthrax Shots," *Whistleblower*, April 2007.

Angie A. Welborn      "Mandatory Vaccinations: Precedent and Current Laws," *CRS Report for Congress*, January 18, 2005. www.fas.org/sgp/crs/RS21414.pdf.

# Index

## A

AAPS (Association of American Physicians & Surgeons, Inc.), 71, 91
Activists (anti-vaccine), 68–73
Adsorbed anthrax vaccination (AVA), 148
Adults, vaccination rates, 154–155
*Adverse Events Associated with Childhood Vaccines* (report), 67
Advisory Committee on Immunization Practices, CDC, 66, 153
Africa
    malaria, 178
    measles, 157–161
    poliovirus, 60
AIDS Community Health Initiative Enroute to A Vaccine Effort (Project Achieve), 170
AIDS vaccine, 28–29, 152, 162 *See also* HIV/AIDS
    experimental, 173–176
    government vaccine, 174
AIDS Vaccine Research Committee, 175
Allergies, 21
American Academy of Pediatrics (AAP), 34, 66, 91, 93
American Cancer Society, 193
*American Journal of Human Genetics,* 72
American Medical Association (AMA), 91
Animal vaccines, 37
Anthrax
    Brachman study, 148–149
    cutaneous, 123, 148
    gastrointestinal, 124
    inhalation, 147–149
    naturally occurring, 147
    terrorism, 119, 122
    types, 123–124
    weaponized, 124
Anthrax vaccination, 29, 89
    allergic reactions, 123
    AVA, 148
    contraindications, 122
    development, 148
    side effects, 123
    Soviet Union, 149
    U.S. military, 120–124, 136–146
    U.S. vaccine, 148
Anti-vaccination activists, 68–73, 77–78
*Archives of General Psychiatry,* 68
*Archives of Pediatrics and Adolescent Medicine,* 61, 93
Associated Press (AP), 40, 76
Association of American Physicians and Surgeons, Inc. (AAPS), 71, 91
Autism, 17, 22–24
    anti-vaccination activists and, 68–70
    California, 32
    genetics, 71–72
    government-funded studies, 42
    New Jersey, 97
    public deception, 46–47
    scientific evidence, 45–47, 69–70
    thimerosal, 28, 37–38
"Autistic Spectrum Disorders, Changes in the California Caseload: 1999–2002" (report), 32

AVA (adsorbed anthrax vaccination), 148

Aventis Pasteur, 35, 39

**B**

*Baltimore Sun* (newspaper), 68

Battelle, 148

Bill and Melinda Gates Foundation, 164, 178

Bioport Corporation, 148

Bioshield Act, 119

Bioterrorism, 119–120

Bookchin, Deborah, 106

Brachman anthrax study, 148–149

British Columbia Cancer Agency, 53

*British Medical Journal,* 68, 91, 98

Brown & Crouppen, 50

Burton, Dan, 37

**C**

California Department of Developmental Services (DDS), 32

California Department of Public Health, 68, 70

California Environmental Protection Agency Office of Environmental Health Hazard Assessment, 99

California Mercury Free Act, 101

*Canadian Medical Association Journal,* 50

Canadian Public Health Agency, 55

Canadian Women's Health Network (CWHN), 52, 54–55

Cancer, 29

Cancer, cancer vaccine
antigen vaccines, 186
CEA-TRICOM vaccine, 187, 191
fowlpox CEA vaccine, 191
immune response, 185–188
licensing, 189–190
PANVAC vaccine, 187
research, 187, 188
standard therapies, 184–185
strategies, 187
treatment, 184
trials, 188, 190–192
whole-cell vaccines, 186

Cancer Center, Duke University, 187–188

Cancer Therapy Evaluation Program, NCI, 188

CEA-TRICOM vaccine, 187, 191

Center for Biologics Evaluation and Research, FDA, 184

Center for Medical Consumers, 89

Center for Vaccine Research, University of Pittsburgh, 22

Centers for Disease Control and Prevention (CDC), 23–24, 27
Advisory Committee on Immunization Practices, 153
disease treatment, estimates, 155
meningitis vaccine and, 81–83
pharmaceutical companies and, 38
thimerosal and, 47

Cervical cancer. *See* human papilloma virus
family-focused groups, 86
Gardasil and, 54–57
rates, 84, 87

Chickenpox (varicella) vaccine, 91–93

Children
CDC recommendations, 64–67
dosages, 38–39
immune systems, 66
New Jersey mandates, 96–103

simultaneous vaccination, 65–66

vaccination rates schedules, 64–65, 111

vaccination rates, schedules, 154

Children's Hospital of Pittsburgh, 22

Children's Hospital, Philadelphia, 40

Chiron Corporation, 101

Christian Scientists, 42

Chronic disease, infectious disease vs., 38–39

The Church of Jesus Christ of Latter-day Saints, 80

*Clinical Infectious Diseases* (journal), 154

Cocharan Collaboration, 98

College students, meningitis vaccination, 81

Combined Joint Unit Task Force-76 (CJUT-76), 122

CWHN (Canadian Women's Health Network), 52, 54–55

Cytos, 195–196

**D**

Dartmouth Medical School, 53

Datamonitor, 110, 112

DDS (California Department of Developmental Services), 32

Department of Health and Human Services (HHS), 26, 38

Department of Preventative Health, Vanderbilt University, 156

*Desert News*, 80

Developing countries, 152–153

Diphtheria-pertussis-tetanus (DPT) vaccination, 27, 35, 65

Dryvax smallpox vaccine, 149

DtaP-Hib, 65

**E**

Eli Lilly and Co., 36

Emory Vaccination Center, 155

*Encyclopedia of Medicine*, 91

Environmental Protection Agency (EPA), 35

Environmental Working Group, 70

*Evidence of Harm—Mercury in Vaccines and the Autism Epidemic* (Kirby), 69

Extraordinary exemptions, 106–107

**F**

Facebook, 50

Family Research Council, 84–85

FDA Summary for Basis of Approval (SBA), 92

FDA (U.S. Food and Drug Administration), 24, 84

Federal Bureau of Investigation (FBI), 119

Fisher, Barbara Leo, 19, 38–39, 43, 78

Flu, 17, 34 *See also* influenza vaccine

Fowlpox CEA vaccine, 191

Freedom of choice, 77–79

**G**

Gardasil, 28, 49
 CDC and, 51
 cervical cancer risk, 54–56
 effectiveness, 84
 Family Research Council, 84–85
 FDA, 51

financial motives, 87–88
Guillian-Barré syndrome and, 50–51
long-term effects, 52–54
medical evidence, 50–52
medical *vs.* moral issues, 85–86
opponents, 85
potential risks, 88–90
religious-right groups, 84–85
side effects, 49
GAVI (Global Alliance for Vaccines and Immunization), 152, 160, 164
GBS (Guillian-Barré syndrome), 50–51, 98
Geier, David, 34
Geier, Mark, 33
Genetic Centers of America, 33
Genetics, autism, 71–72
GenVec Inc., 174
GeoVax Labs Inc., 173–176
Ghrelin, 195
GlaxoSmithKline (GSK), 53, 180
Global Alliance for Vaccines and Immunization (GAVI), 152, 160, 164
Government response, 50
Governmental powers, 104–109
conflicting values, 133–135
critics, 129–130
historical, 131
individual *vs.* collective interests, 131–135
justification, 130–132
planning provisions, 128
proposed, 127–130
public health emergency and, 131
restriction, intervention, 129
standards, 132–133
surveillance, 128

terrorism and, 125–135
tolerance, 133
Government-funded studies, 42
GSK (GlaxoSmithKline), 53
Guillian-Barré syndrome (GBS), 50–51, 98
Gulf War Syndrome, 29, 120

**H**

H. Lee Moffit Cancer Center and Research Institute, 189
*Healthfacts* (newsletter), 89
Heart disease, 34
Herd immunity, 105–106
HHS (Department of Health and Human Services), 26, 38
Hib-HepB (hepatitis B), 65
HIV preventive vaccine trials, 165–173
adverse effects, 167
confidentiality, 168
cultural differences, 170
education, 167–169
gender recognition, 170
informed consent, 167–168
participation barriers, 169
participation benefits, 169–171
physical setting, 168
recruitment efforts, 170
research, 172
retention rates, 170–171
sample group, 170
sex workers, 168–169, 171
social risks, 169
tenofovir, 171
treatment, 162
vaccine trial protocols, 171
women's concerns, 165–167
HIV Vaccine Trials Network, 175

HIV/AIDS
    activists, 163–164
    children, 162–164
    government-funded studies, 174
    human rights, 171
    Merck STEP study, 173, 175
    Phambili trial, 176
    pneumonia vaccine, 163–164
    pre-exposure prophylaxis trials, 171
    rates, 163
Hoffman, Stephen, 181–183
Homeland security, 125
*Huffington Post* (web site), 114
Human papilloma virus (HPV), 17 *See also* Gardasil
    cervical cancer and, 56–57
    pharmaceutical companies and, 112

**I**

IDSA (Infectious Diseases Society of America), 154–156
Immune response, cancer, 185–188
Immunization programs, 62, 76
Immunization Services Division, CDC, 41
*Immunotherapy Weekly*, 93
Imus, Deirdre, 114–115
Imus, Don, 42
Individual *vs.* collective interests, 19, 131–135
Infectious diseases
    chronic disease *vs.*, 38–39
    deaths, 23
    developing countries, 152–153
    resurgence, 61–62, 72
    vectors, 22
Infectious Diseases Society of America (IDSA), 154–156

Influenza vaccine, 34, 98–100, 115
*Insight* (journal), 35–36, 38
Institute of Medicine (IOM), 33, 47, 67
International AIDS Vaccine Initiative, 168, 174
Internet, 16–17

**J**

*Jacobsen v. Commonwealth of Massachusetts*, 18
Jenner, Edward, 58, 79
John Hopkins University Bloomberg School of Public Health, 154
*Journal of American Medical Association* (JAMA), 17, 116
*Journal of American Physicians and Surgeons*, 33
*Journal of Child Neurology*, 99
*Journal of Pediatrics*, 99
Judicial Watch, 51

**K**

Kennedy, Robert, 70
Kirby, David, 69

**L**

Laboratory of Tumor Immunology and Biology, NCI, 184
*Lancet* (journal), 163
Live-virus vaccination, 27–28
*Los Angles Times* (newspaper), 119

**M**

*Maclean's* (magazine), 50
Malaria, 152, 177
    Africa, 178
    Bush (G.W.) Administration, 178–179

GlaxoSmithKline Biologicals, 180
  Hoffman, 181–183
  research teams, 180–182
  RTS, S vaccine, 180
  Sanaria, 181–183
  threat, 178–179
  vaccine development, 179–180
  vaccine funding, 164
Maternal Nutrition Group, 71
McCarthy, Jenny, 71
Measles
  accelerate control strategies, 161
  Africa, 157–158, 160–161
  age-specific rates, 160
  anti-body levels, children, 159
  complications, 160
  emergence, 157
  fatality ratios, 157–158
  global mortality decline, 159–160
  recent outbreaks, 160–161
  susceptibility, 157
Measles Initiative, 160
Measles-mumps-rubella (MMR) vaccination, 36–37, 65, 158–159
Mecon Inc., 34
Medical exemptions, 108
Medical research, 17
Medical vs. moral, 85–86
Meningitis vaccination
  college students, 81–83
  community risk, 82–83
  mandatory, 81–82
  side effects, 82–83
Meningococcal vaccine, 98
Merck & Co., Inc., 84, 173–175
  financial motives, 87–88
  Gardisal trials, 89–90, 111
  lobbying, 88
Merck Frosst Canada Ltd., 51

Mercury, 24, 29, 34 See also thimerosal
  amounts, 115
  autism, 37–38
  influenza vaccine, 115
  safety guidelines, 33–34
  toxicity, 97–98
Mercury Free Act, 101
MMR (measles-mumps-rubella) vaccination, 36–37, 65, 158–159
Moalem, Sharon, 55
Mount Sinai School of Medicine, 55

N

National Academy of Sciences Institute of Medicine (IOM), 33, 47, 67
National and Global Public Health Committee, IDSA, 156
National Cancer Institute (NCI), 184
National Institute of Allergy and Infectious Diseases, 194
National Institute on Drug Abuse, 193
National Institutes of Health (NIH), 24
National Organization for Rare Disorders, 190
National Toxicology Program (NTP), 99
National Vaccine Advisory Committee, 156
National Vaccine Information Center, 43, 78, 89
National Vaccine Injury Compensation Program, 26, 69
Naval Medical Research Center, 181
NCI (National Cancer Institute), 184

*Neuroendochronology Letters* (journal), 24

Neurological disorders, 24–25, 33

*New England Journal of Medicine,* 54, 113

New Jersey
autism rates, 97
PHC, 96
vaccine mandates, 94–103

*New York Times* (newspaper), 69, 89, 181

*NewsMax* (web site), 112–113

Nicotine vaccine, 194–197

NicVAX, 196

NIH (National Institutes of Health), 24

NTP (National Toxicology Program), 99

**O**

Obesity vaccine, 195

*Oprah* (television), 71

Oregon Health Science University (OHSU), 113

OSHU (Oregon Health Science University), 113

"Over Medicated and Over-Vaccinated" (article), 114

Over-vaccination, 114–117

**P**

Package labeling, 35–37

PANVAC vaccine, 187

Pap smears, 56, 88

Paraguay, 153

Parents, 21–22, 39, 41
informed consent, 108–109
medical neglect, 108–109
motivation, 62
organizations, 115

PDR *(Physicians' Desk Reference),* 35

Pediatric Infectious Diseases, University of Utah, 156

*Pediatrics* (journal), 62

Pennsylvania, 22

Perinatal HIV Research Unit, Chris Hani Baragwanath Hospital, 176

Personal liberty, 125–135

Pertussis, 26, 30, 59–60 *See also* diphtheria-pertussis-tetanus vaccine

Pfizer, 102

Phambili trial, 176

Pharmaceutical industry, 102
CDC and, 38
HHS and, 38
HPV and, 112
market size, sales, 110–112

PHC (Public Health Council), 96

Philosophical exemptions, 43–44, 77

*Physicians' Desk Reference* (PDR), 35, 94

Physicians, patients, 156

"Pipeline and Commercial Insight: Pediatric and Adolescent Vaccines" (report), 110

*Playboy* (magazine), 71

*PLoS Medicine* (journal), 157, 160

Pneumococcal vaccine, 100, 164

Pneumonia, HIV-positive children, 162–164

Polio vaccine, 27–28, 28

Polio vaccine, Africa, 60

Poliovirus, 60

Prevnar, 100, 111

Project Achieve (AIDS Community Health Initiative Enroute to A Vaccine Effort), 170

Public Health Agency, Canada, 55
Public health authorities, 18–19, 30
Public Health Council (PHC), New Jersey, 96
Public health, individual rights *vs.*, 19
Public Health Service Act, Section 317, 155
PutChildrenFirst.org, 115–116

**R**

Redwood, Lyn, 116
Religious beliefs, 40, 42–43, 84
Religious exemptions, 19, 21
    rates, 40–41, 76
    states, 41–42
Resistant bacteria, 112–114
Risk assessment, 104
Rodewald, Lance, 41
Rosenberg, Steven, 186
RotaTeq, 112
RTS, S malaria vaccine, 180
Rubella, 58, 60–61

**S**

SafeMinds, 116
Salk, Jonas, 60
Sanaria, 181–183
Sanofi Aventis, 98
SARS (severe acute respiratory syndrome), 32
SBA (Summary for Basis of Approval, FDA), 92
Schechter, Robert, 70
Schlom, Jeffrey, 184
Schumacher, Jim, 106
Scripps Research Institute, 197
Section 317, Public Health Service Act, 155

Severe acute respiratory syndrome (SARS), 32
Seymour Johnson Air Force Base, N.C., 136
Simian virus 40 (SV40), 29
Smallpox, 60–61, 79, 120
Smallpox vaccination, 149
    Dryvax, 149
    immunity duration, 114
    production, 149
    side effects, 149
Smokers, 194–197
Soviet Union, anthrax vaccination, 149
State requirements, 41–44, 76, 105–106
STEP study, 173
Summary for Basis of Approval (SBA), FDA, 92
*Survival of the Sickest* (Moalem), 55
SV40 (Simian virus 40), 29

**T**

"Technical Report: Mercury in the Environment: Implications for Pediatricians," 99
Tenofovir, 171
Terrorism
    active surveillance, 128
    anthrax, 119
    government planning provisions, 128
    governmental powers, 125–135
    homeland security, 125
    risk of attack, 126–127
    smallpox, 120
    surveillance provisions, 128
    vaccination effectiveness, 150
Tetanus. *See* diphtheria-pertussis-tetanus vaccine

Texas, HPV vaccine, 88
Therion Biologic, 191
Thimerosal, 33, 68–69
 AAP, 99
 autism and, 28, 37–38
 CDC and, 47
 heart disease, 34
 *Journal of Pediatrics*, 99
 public deception, 46–47
 scientific evidence, 45–47, 69–70
 vaccine component, 35–36
"Thimerosal in Childhood Vaccines, Neurodevelopmental Disorders and Heart Disease in the United States" (study), 34
Toxins, 24
Transdisciplinary Tobacco Use Research Center, 197
Trivalent IPV, 65
Tuberculosis, vaccine funding, 164

## U

U.K. Health Department, 62
University of Maryland School of Medicine, 114
University of Minnesota Cancer Center, 197
University of Wisconsin-Madison Hospitals and Clinics, 113
U.S. Court of Federal Claims, 100
U.S. Department of Defense, 147
U.S. Department of Education, 32
U.S. Food and Drug Administration (FDA), 24
U.S. Food and Drug Administration (FDA), 24, 84
U.S. military, anthrax vaccine, 120–124, 136–146
U.S. Public Health Service, 34, 113
USA VaxGen, 148

Utah
 The Church of Jesus Christ of Latter-day Saints, 80
 smallpox, 79–80
 vaccination opposition, 79–80
Utah Valley Regional Medical Center, 76

## V

Vaccine Adverse Effects Reporting System (VAERS), 49
Vaccine Research Center, 175
Vaccine Research Center, National Institute of Allergy and Infectious Diseases, 194
Vaccine safety database (VSD), 47
Vaccines and Related Biologic Products Advisory Committee, FDA, 89
Vaccines, vaccination *See also* specific types
 advocates, 104
 animal, 37
 arguments against, 75
 childhood schedule, 64–65, 111
 children, 38–39
 children, CDC recommendation, 64–67
 children *vs.* adults, 154–156
 combination, 64–67
 compliance, 18
 compulsory, 18–19, 21, 27, 76, 81–82, 92–94, 104–117, 123–124, 147
 coverage rates, 106
 debate, 17–18, 26–27
 developing countries, 152–153
 duration, 113–114
 effectiveness, 77, 150
 future, 152–153
 industry, 110
 infectious disease and, 58–59

ingredients, 32–33
live-virus, 26
medical exemptions, 108
medical *vs.* moral, 85–86
multiple, 64–67
new, 28–30, 110–117
New Jersey, 94, 96–103
new technology, 194–196
non-medical exemptions, 61
parasitic disease, 179
preschool, 85, 99–100
promotion, 154
resistance, 40–41
risk *vs.* benefit, 58–63
sales, 101–102
simultaneous, 65–66
state power, 105–106
supporters, 17
(VAERS) Vaccine Adverse Effects
  Reporting System, 49
Vical Inc., 174
Vioxx, 89
*The Virus and the Vaccine*
  (Bookchin, Schumacher), 106
VSD (vaccine safety database), 47

**W**

*WebM* (e-zine), 70
Weldon, Dave, 100
Whooping cough. *See* pertussis
Winfrey, Oprah, 71
*WND (World Net Daily)*, 28–29
Women, HIV preventive vaccine
  trials, 165–172
Women in Government, 88
World Health Organization
  (WHO), 153, 178
*World Net Daily (WND)*, 28–29
Wyeth, 100, 111

**Y**

Yellow fever, 153
YouTube, 16–17

**Z**

Zogby International, 115